A SHORT
HISTORY
of the
WORLD *in*
50 FAILURES

Also in the series:

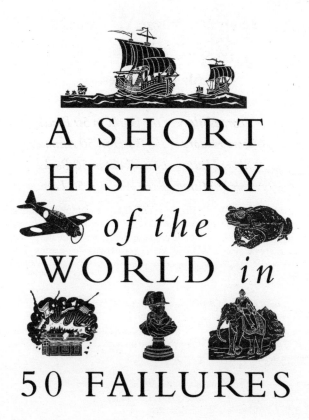

A SHORT HISTORY *of the* WORLD *in* 50 FAILURES

Ben Gazur

Illustrated by Becca Thorne

Michael O'Mara Books Limited

To my best friend Nic Attwood,
who has never failed me.

First published in Great Britain in 2024 by
Michael O'Mara Books Limited
9 Lion Yard
Tremadoc Road
London SW4 7NQ

A CIP catalogue record for this book is available from the British Library.

Papers used by Michael O'Mara Books Limited are natural, recyclable products made from wood grown in sustainable forests. The manufacturing processes conform to the environmental regulations of the country of origin.

ISBN: 978-1-78929-693-8 in hardback print format
ISBN: 978-1-78929-708-9 in trade paperback format
ISBN: 978-1-78929-694-5 in ebook format

2 3 4 5 6 7 8 9 10

Designed and typeset by Claire Cater
Illustrations by Becca Thorne
Printed and bound by CPI Group (UK) Ltd, Croydon, CR0 4YY
www.mombooks.com

CONTENTS

INTRODUCTION

INTRODUCTION – ON THE NATURE OF FAILURE

. . . .

Success is everywhere. It is the loud-mouthed passenger on public transport who just does not know when to shut up. You cannot escape it. If you open social media you will be inundated with stories and images that chronicle every single success in people's lives. Books, television and cinema abound with tales of people overcoming obstacles and finally reaching the top. We are a success society in which failure, be it big or small, is viewed with suspicion and fear – as if the taint of misfortune might be contagious. It is time to sing the praises of failure.

There has been a tendency to view history as a never-ending series of brilliant successes. Grand tomes trace the path of science from simple beginnings to unravelling the fundamental mysteries of nature. In medicine, we have gone from invoking the gods as an explanation for disease to curing illnesses that were previously a death sentence. Everyone enjoys epic accounts of leaders who have accumulated victories to conquer expansive empires, but what these self-congratulatory histories miss is that failure has played just as great a role in shaping the human story.

Throughout history, many individuals tagged as failures have played their part in shaping our world, and most fall into a few basic categories. There is the heroic failure who tried something no one had ever done before. Yes, they failed, but they inspired others to try. Then there are those who, by trying to achieve one thing, fail so badly they end up accomplishing something else, completely unexpectedly. There are other failures where a policy was meant to change something but had utterly unforeseen consequences. Sometimes a failure is just a missed opportunity, where the smallest mistake snatched failure from the jaws of glory.

Everyone has experienced at least some failure in their lives. We try to cover it up as best as possible, to present ourselves only as we would like to be seen by the world, but in our hearts we all know we are failures in some way or other. It is understandable that most histories tend not to dwell on failure, as humans are failure-averse. The whole story of our species is incomplete, however, if we do not acknowledge the failures that have landed us where we are today.

This book, if it is not an utter failure in its aim, will examine some of the most consequential failures that have dogged human endeavours. We will see nations rise from the ashes of a blunder, people who failed to recognize their chance to win, and even those few spectacular failures that created the perfect conditions to usher in new worlds of discovery.

There may be depressing failures in this book and a great deal of misfortune, but there should at least be a glimmer of hope. Once you see how terribly some people have messed things up, you will understand that things can always be worse.

Part I

THE ANCIENT WORLD

HUMAN COUSINS FAIL TO SURVIVE

A modern visitor to Europe sixty-five thousand years ago would find the trappings of a thriving culture already in place. Communities who lived there used red ochre for decoration, created jewellery from shells and bones, and used fire to light caves, in which they also left evidence of their creativity. Some cave walls are covered in dots, wavy lines and other designs that would not look out of place in an art gallery today.

These people gathered resources from the environment

and used them in complex ways. By burning birchbark near a flat rock, they were able to scrape off a resin that could be employed in everything from making weapons, to treating leather, to disinfection. Stone tools have been discovered that were made to a remarkable level of sophistication, and wooden spears were probably also used to bring down prey many times the hunters' own size.

When an individual was injured, they would have been cared for by other members of their tribe. The scars of degenerative diseases and healed wounds still visible on skeletons show that even those who were unable to contribute for long periods received food and help from those around them. And when they died, they could hope to be placed in a grave by those they left behind.

All of this might seem unsurprising. It is no less than we have come to expect from humans with their propensity to form societies, express artistic flair and exploit technologies – except that sixty-five thousand years ago there were no modern humans in Europe. These discoveries all relate to Neanderthals.

There are no Neanderthals alive today because modern humans, *Homo sapiens*, have replaced them. How is it that our ancestors triumphed in the battle for survival and the Neanderthals failed?

The road to human dominance over the Earth only seems

smooth to us because we are the end product of millions of years of survival stories. This idea of human evolution is best exemplified by the image known as 'The March of Progress', which shows a progression of human ancestors starting with chimp-like apes and ending with a modern man striding into the future. Unfortunately, this image has given generations of students the notion that modern humans are the pinnacle of evolution.

Our ancestors are just those individuals who lived long enough to leave enough offspring to carry on their genes, but many others were not so lucky. That road, which appears to lead directly to us, actually had many dangerous turns and dead ends. Today, there is only one branch on the human family tree, but extinct species that were closely related to us are being discovered by palaeontologists all the time.

Scientists debate exactly how many hominin species existed at various times in the past, but it is certain that many of them held huge evolutionary potential. Each was well suited to the environment it developed in, and, for tens of thousands of years, each could boast of being the dominant hominin in their domain. One by one, they all went extinct, except for our ancestors.

Homo floresiensis was a diminutive species of hominin that inhabited the island of Flores in modern Indonesia around a hundred thousand years ago. Standing just a metre tall, they would have looked small to us, but their smaller stature made them better able to adapt to the limited resources of their island home. Yet, even with dramatic evolutionary advantages, the little people of Flores died out around fifty thousand years ago. It is likely no coincidence that this is around the same time that *Homo sapiens* arrived in the area.

Neanderthals survived in Europe until around thirty thousand years ago, in increasingly isolated regions. No longer could they roam the continent as they used to because populations of modern humans had begun to inhabit the lands on which Neanderthals had depended. The Neanderthals may have looked like humans, behaved like humans in many respects, and been stronger in certain other ways, but modern humans survived and the Neanderthals did not.

Neanderthals were in no way stupid, but they do seem to have lacked the versatility that meant *Homo sapiens* was able to master all the lands it entered. When climates shifted, our ancestors may have been more adaptable. It may be that our ancestors were simply better able to gather resources, and the Neanderthals were unable to compete. Or perhaps our ancestors killed the Neanderthals. The failure of our cousin species may have been key to the rise of humanity.

Before humans become too proud of their achievement of outlasting their relatives, it must be noted that *Homo sapiens* came very close to being just another of the lost hominin species. Around a hundred thousand years ago, the ancestors of modern humans passed through what is known as the Human Genetic Bottleneck. By studying the DNA of humans across the world, scientists have calculated that we very nearly went extinct. Just one thousand two hundred human ancestors were alive at this time, and all modern humans are closely related to them.

If there had been just one more bad winter, a terrible storm, or a volcanic eruption, then there would be no

Homo sapiens alive today, and modern Neanderthals could be left wondering how it was that our ancestors failed when theirs survived.

VOICES FROM THE PAST

Scientists debate whether Neanderthals had the anatomical ability to speak. Some suggest that their inability to communicate as easily as *Homo sapiens* contributed to their extinction. Other researchers believe they could make the same range of sounds as modern humans, but we will never know what they said.

INDUS VALLEY CIVILIZATION COLLAPSES

. . . .

The cities of the Indus Valley civilization are among the wonders of the ancient world. These remarkable urban centres flourished around 2000 BC and are markedly different from the cities of Egypt and Mesopotamia that existed at the time.

Egypt might boast mountainous pyramids and Mesopotamia its temples, but the Indus Valley cities are strikingly modern in ways that other civilizations of the day were not.

Many sites from the ancient world are famous because of the remaining monumental architecture created to honour a powerful ruler or deity, but there are few constructions of this type from the cities of the Indus Valley civilization of the Bronze Age. Stretching from modern Pakistan to Afghanistan and into north-west India, dozens of settlements from this period have been uncovered.

The first such city to be discovered, Harappa, exemplifies what could be found at most Indus Valley sites. Tens of thousands of people lived in an urbanized community with flat-roofed houses made from either mud or fired clay bricks. At Harappa, all of the houses were connected to both fresh water and sewage systems far more advanced than those seen in most cities for millennia. Brick waste bins were even constructed at strategic points to allow people to dispose of litter without fouling the streets.

The cities were supported by the agricultural hinterlands, which kept the citizens well fed and allowed them to pursue other forms of industry such as cloth-spinning, metalwork, pottery, stone carving and shipbuilding. With artisans producing high-quality goods, trade between the Indus cities thrived. Warehouses, wharfs and way stations have been discovered from this time that kept products flowing between cities. The food grown by the farmers was exported widely, and raw materials were imported across long distances. For example, agate was brought into the Indus Valley from hundreds of kilometres away, then turned into luxurious beads and the stone seals found at almost every site.

There are several things missing from Indus Valley cities that archaeologists might have expected. Where are the grand palace complexes of their kings? Where are the soaring temples? No unambiguously royal or religious sites have yet been discovered. This has led some to imagine the Indus Valley civilization as an egalitarian, atheist utopia shaped by socialist ideals. It was once thought, too, that its inhabitants were pacifists, as, unlike most ancient civilizations, their art did not depict warfare.

Understanding the nature of life in the Indus Valley is made more difficult as we have no idea of their political organization. Was each city run by an oligarchy? Were the cities united in some way other than by culture? Were they rivals? Did they go to war with each other? The archaeologists who have worked at these sites have found skeletons marked by the sort of wounds inflicted during battle, and metal spears and arrowheads are well represented. Warfare, if it did occur, was probably limited to small-scale raids rather than large pitched engagements. The entire Indus Valley region was separated by natural barriers from the powerful enemies who might have been able to launch an invasion.

With all this said, it seems that the Indus Valley civilization should have waxed into a prosperous and enduring state, but this is not what the archaeology reveals. Around 1900 BC, the great cities of the Indus Valley began to show signs of failure. Housing became crowded, and building quality declined. The important drainage systems were blocked and never repaired. In a matter of two centuries, it seems as if the whole civilization vanished.

Archaeologists are beginning to unravel the mystery of the failure of the Indus Valley civilization, though there is no consensus. Early theories suggested invasion from an outside power, but no evidence for this has been found. It is likely the Indus Valley cities fell due to forces beyond their control. One of their trading partners, the Akkadian civilization of Mesopotamia, was suffering from a period of prolonged drought and increasingly arid conditions around this time, and their king lists show a confusion of rulers who emerged and were deposed after short reigns. Trade with the Indus Valley fell away as the cities of Mesopotamia squabbled, and, without imported materials, the artisans of the Indus Valley could no longer produce their usual goods. The traders no longer had the means to support themselves.

The Indus Valley was also undergoing its own climatic shifts. Cities could only feed themselves and import goods if they had access to a river, so that, when one dried up, it removed both a trade route and a source of water. The Ghaggar-Hakra River was supplied through the inundations brought by monsoons, but when the frequency of these rains diminished the whole river dried up, only appearing occasionally when monsoons did strike.

Studies of lake sediments have revealed that this dry period may have lasted for nine hundred years. This prolonged drought would have brought profound changes to agriculture. The dense and urbanized cities could no longer be fed by their farmers. The large public works, like the Great Bath of Mohenjo-Daro, were expensive luxuries when people were struggling to feed themselves. By 1700 BC, most of the cities of the Indus Valley were abandoned, and the cultural achievements of their civilization were lost for thousands of years.

The cities were left derelict, but villages sprang up bearing many of the same artistic styles found at the height of the civilization's power. People do not meekly cling to their homes when times get tough. Faced with impossible situations in their cities, it seems they moved into the countryside to smaller polities that could support them. This was evolution and not collapse, according to many archaeologists.

Climate change has long shaped the history of humanity. The lesson of the past is that those who do not adapt die.

A BROKEN BEAUTY

A grand necklace made from precious stones, jade, agate and gold beads found in Mohenjo-Daro was held up as one of the Indus Valley civilization's greatest artworks. In the bloody partition of India and Pakistan, it was decided that each new state should be given a portion of the necklace.

AKHENATEN FOUNDS A NEW RELIGION NO ONE LIKES

People talk of the vast span of ancient Egyptian civilization as if it were static, unchanging and impervious to the vicissitudes of history. Even as far back as the life of the ancient Greek philosopher Plato in the fourth and fifth centuries BC, many regarded Egypt as the model of stability in a state and a storehouse of antediluvian wisdom. It is easy to see why this impression developed. When we look at a temple wall, whether it is from 3000 BC or the Roman period of the second century AD, there is a superficial uniformity in style that suggests no developments ever occurred.

Those who have studied the history of Egypt, however, know that it was a state subject to the fates of all nations. There were invasions, civil wars, plotting by rival factions and disasters. These events are known through their written history, carved in hieroglyphs, and recorded in the archaeology. When archaeologists uncover new sites they can sometimes force us to reconsider what we thought we knew of life in Egypt. No single site did this as dramatically as Amarna, which proved to be a monument to the revolutionary life and failed religious programme of the pharaoh Akhenaten.

In the nineteenth century, the ruins of a city at Amarna were mapped by European visitors, and it was soon noted that the art springing from the sands was radically different from that found in the rest of Egypt. At Amarna, the stylized figures on reliefs have long, exaggerated limbs often held in fluid poses, quite unlike the stiff rigidity of poses in many other Egyptian carvings. Most notably, the images of people have heads that are elongated with large features. In many

of the artworks uncovered, Akhenaten is depicted beneath a radiant sun, its beams ending in hands that offer a blessing.

The image of the sun is key to understanding Akhenaten. He took the throne of Egypt as Amenhotep IV on the death of his father, around 1352 BC. The evidence from his early reign shows Amenhotep IV fulfilling all the usual functions of the Egyptian pharaoh, such as worshipping the traditional gods of the Egyptian pantheon. Monuments and inscriptions set up by his subjects continued to follow a traditional style of art and to honour the gods as they had always done.

There was, however, a shift towards a new focus on religious veneration. Amenhotep IV supported the building of temples for the gods, but many from his early reign were dedicated to the god Aten. The disc of the sun was Aten's image, which was somewhat unusual, as most of the Egyptian gods were anthropomorphic – even with animalistic aspects such as crocodile heads, they resembled their human worshippers. It was Aten who Amenhotep IV chose to exult above all other gods.

In the fifth year of his reign, Amenhotep IV decreed Aten supreme god of the pantheon. The foundations of a new capital, named Akhetaten in the god's honour, were laid. The pharaoh also changed his name to Akhenaten, meaning something like 'of great use to Aten', or 'effective for Aten'. The rest of the royal family also took names that referred to Aten, such as Meritaten and Tutankhaten. As Akhenaten, the pharaoh set about ensuring that only his god would be worshipped – archaeologists have discovered inscriptions with the names of other gods chiselled out.

The nature of Atenism, as the new faith of Akhenaten is known, is hotly debated by scholars, but it seems fairly clear that it was one of the first monotheistic religions in human history. The *Great Hymn to the Aten* describes him as the 'sole god', creating all of the world on his own. While the old gods had a physical form that was represented in temples throughout the country, there was a sense in which Aten was everywhere at all times. He was the light of the sun, and everything that saw the light was blessed by Aten.

This was not to be an egalitarian faith, however. One person especially benefited from the special patronage of Aten, and that was his greatest follower, Akhenaten. In the strange new art of Atenism, the rays of the sun pass through most people and objects, but they surround and anoint the royal family. It was Akhenaten who greeted the rising sun each morning. On special days, the statues of the gods had once been paraded through the streets, but now it was Akhenaten who rode in a chariot to receive the praise of worshippers on Aten's behalf. Aten may have blessed the whole world, but he seemed to pay special attention to Akhenaten. Indeed, Akhenaten decreed that only he was able to worship Aten. If the people wanted access to their one god, they had to go through their one priest.

The central role of Akhenaten in Atenism has led some Egyptologists to theorize that this revolutionary new religion was created less out of divine inspiration and more out of a lust for power. The priesthoods of the Egyptian gods were powerful both spiritually and politically, as, with their special access to the gods, they alone claimed the right to interpret divine will, and it was prudent for the pharaohs to do as they said. The temple complexes governed by the priests also had access to vast resources. By closing the temples and casting out priests while making himself the sole interpreter of the supreme god's dictates, Akhenaten took full control of his kingdom.

The final years of Akhenaten's reign are poorly understood. There is some evidence that a plague may have struck Egypt during this period, but even that is not certain. All we can say is that Akhenaten died in the seventeenth year of his reign, and the downfall of Atenism came soon afterwards.

Within two years of Tutankhaten taking the throne, the shift back to the traditional gods had begun. Tutankhaten renamed himself Tutankhamun, to honour the god Amun, and moved the capital to Memphis. An inscription set up under Tutankhamun described how disastrous the flirtation with Aten had been, saying that temples had been left to rot and the gods had turned deaf ears to their supplicants. The Temples of Aten and the great new capital of Akhetaten were dismantled and their stones reused to build shrines and temples for other gods.

Under the pharaohs that followed, an attempt was made to scrub away all references to Akhenaten and his interloping god. Akhenaten was described by later Egyptians simply as 'the enemy'.

The faith of Atenism, whether it was a bold step towards monotheism or a naked grab for absolute power, was a failure. If archaeologists had not uncovered Akhetaten, then no one would ever have known that, for a brief few years, only a single god shone down on Egypt.

NO REST FOR THE WICKED

While Tutankhamun's tomb was full of 'wonderful things', the tomb of Akhenaten was abandoned along with his new city. The sarcophagus that Akhenaten was first laid in was broken up, and his mummified remains were removed. It is likely that these were transported to a tomb in the Valley of the Kings. Even there he did not long rest in peace, as his tomb was ransacked later in antiquity.

THE BRONZE AGE COLLAPSE

The late Bronze Age around the Eastern Mediterranean, around 1700 to 900 BC, was a time of prosperity for many civilizations. Trade boomed as ships carried tin and copper across the sea, caravans carried valuable commodities over long distances, and writing systems developed to record accounts for merchants and kings.

On Crete, the Minoans built palace complexes, to which were brought crops and products that were then distributed to people under a central authority. This palace economy can also be found in the Mycenaean societies of the Greek mainland. It is thought that these palaces were constructed by powerful local kings or warriors to govern their domains and cement their authority, by giving them control of supplies. The writing left on artefacts from Crete led to hopes of the discovery of an unknown corpus of grand literary texts that might prefigure the tales of Homer. When the code of Linear B was cracked, however, it was found mostly to list goods such as sheep, grain and oil. For historians, this record of how materials passed between people was nearly as exciting as any epic, for it revealed the complex web of supply and demand in the ancient world.

We have evidence of diplomacy between ancient civilizations at this time that highlights the evolution of the nations. After the Battle of Kadesh in 1274 BC, the Hittite Empire and the Egyptians agreed to the first known peace treaty between two nations in recorded history. The versions written in the Hittite language and Egyptian hieroglyphics still exist.

Yet in just a few short years, around the year 1170 BC, the

Greeks, Hittites and Egyptians had all suffered catastrophic failures. The records of the Hittites describe political instability and a devastating plague that killed several of their kings. We also have letters written by Hittite rulers from the twelfth century BC asking the Egyptian pharaohs to send food, as there was 'no grain' in their domain. What we know of the last days of the Hittite Empire comes in part because of its violence. The fires that raged as towns were sacked and abandoned baked their written clay tablets hard enough to survive the millennia.

Recent scientific findings point to a long-lasting change in Bronze Age weather patterns, which would have disrupted agriculture. Drought led directly to famine for several years, pushing the Hittites far beyond what trade and traditional techniques could mitigate. We also know that similar climatic convulsions were occurring across Northern Europe, unleashing the most destructive phase of what is known as the Late Bronze Age collapse.

In Egyptian inscriptions, invaders from unknown locations, whom scholars refer to as the Sea Peoples, are described as descending on Egypt like a natural disaster. They speak of a confederation of people whom no other nation could withstand. The Sea Peoples came in ships, raiding and destroying centres of civilization down the coast of the Eastern Mediterranean. It may be that people from further north in Europe migrated south after famine in their own homelands caused by the worsening of the climate.

Archaeological investigations show that palaces throughout the Greek world were being abandoned around this time. Some were brought down by earthquakes; others were burned. It cannot be said for certain that it was the Sea Peoples who caused the failure of the Greek societies. Some have suggested that when the central power of kings in Greece began to falter due to famine and falling trade, the people they ruled over rose up and cast down the palaces that were symbols of monarchical rule. Some of the Sea Peoples were probably Greeks who had abandoned their ancestral lands themselves, in search of more fertile shores.

On Cyprus, the ruins of Hala Sultan Tekke that date from this period offer compelling evidence of active warfare. An arrowhead was found still stuck in a wall, and lead pellets, used in slings, were scattered all over the ground. Valuable items had been buried, their owners having never returned to retrieve them.

The city of Ugarit in modern Syria was a major trading hub in antiquity, but was ruined by invasion. Letters from the King of Ugarit, calling for aid, paint a vivid portrait of the confusion at the time. The letters describe how the king had sent his army into Hittite territory to try to stem the flow of invaders from the north, yet more raiders were coming from the sea. A final text describes how, by the time aid arrived, Ugarit had been sacked, their food burned, and the people dispersed.

LETTERS FROM THE BRINK

The textual evidence for the invasion of the Sea Peoples left in Ugaritic letters is tragic to read. We learn of people refusing to flee because it would leave their families defenceless. The wealthy were said to tremble in their palaces, while the poor were torn to pieces. The final letter from Ugarit, addressed to a lord, records the ruin of the city. It ends with a plaintive cry for their suffering to be remembered: 'May you know it!'

Many sites, such as the capital of the Hittite Empire at Hattusa, where monumental lions guard one of its main gates, might have been deserted by the time the migration of the Sea Peoples reached Anatolia. With no strong kingdom to stop the advance of the Sea Peoples, they passed ever further south. In Egypt, the records of Ramesses III tell us how raiders from the sea boldly sailed into his territory. In a typically laudatory inscription, we are told how the pharaoh fell on them like a lion, with the ferocity of a whirlwind, and sank the ships of the Sea Peoples so that their weapons lay scattered on the seabed. In a separate battle, the migration of the Sea Peoples via a land route into Egypt was stopped.

The aftermath of the Bronze Age Collapse saw the Hittite Empire utterly destroyed and Greek society cast into what historians refer to as the Dark Age. The palace complexes were never rebuilt, and villages became the main form of polity. The south of Greece underwent severe depopulation, and the majority of sites that had been inhabited in the previous years were left deserted. The writing system that had been used to administer supplies was forgotten, and for hundreds of years nothing was written down.

Whether the Sea Peoples caused the Bronze Age collapse or were just another symptom of it, there is no doubting that societies in Europe at this time lost many of their most advanced features.

FAILURE TO STOP LEAVES FALLING
IN WATER CAUSES A TRADE WAR

· ·

Mythic failures can have real-world consequences that shape nations, economies and provoke wars. Few failures from legend have been more influential than the accidental discovery of tea.

According to Chinese tales, it was Shennong who first tasted the marvels of a good cup of tea. Shennong is credited as either an emperor or a divine figure. Many advances in farming are attributed to him, such as harnessing horses and oxen, and the invention of carts and hoes. The revolution in agriculture that resulted from these innovations freed the Chinese from constant fear of famine, leading to a dramatic increase in the population and the development of stable governments. It is unlikely that one person really made all these breakthroughs, but Shennong remains a revered figure for millions.

According to one version of events, it was in 2737 BC, when Shennong was on campaign with his army, that he ordered water be brought to him. Shennong often boiled his water, either for ritual purity or to avoid illness, and so it was that a servant was carrying a cup of hot water to his master when the wind disturbed a tree and several leaves fell into the cup. When Shennong tasted the water, he was amazed and ordered that more of those fragrant leaves be gathered – and the cultivation of tea was born.

A second version of the story has Shennong boiling water over a fire he had kindled with twigs from a tea tree. The heat of the fire sent leaves from the twigs up into the air before they fell back into the cauldron of water. There, the leaves steeped and created the first pot of tea.

Another variant about the discovery of tea helps to explain the popularity of tea in both Chinese culture and medicine.

Shennong was apparently an experimentalist, as he is reputed to have personally tested hundreds of substances for their potential medical benefits. One day he had consumed seventy-two herbs and found them all to be toxic, but discovered that consuming tea cured him completely. Tea became a mainstay of medical practice for centuries afterwards, though, of course, people also came to appreciate its exquisite taste and the revitalizing effects of its caffeine.

Reliable historical accounts of tea drinking can be traced to at least the third century AD, but plant material discovered in the tomb of Emperor Jing from the second century BC points to tea being drunk at least that far back in history. It appears that it was regarded as a mostly medicinal drink until the Tang dynasty. In the eighth century, Lu Yu wrote *The Classic of Tea*, which discussed everything from the origin of tea to its cultivation and ways of enjoying it. From China, the pleasures of tea spread to Japan and Korea.

Buddhist monks found that drinking tea helped them stay awake during their meditations. This may explain another legendary origin of tea. It is said that the monk Bodhidharma managed to meditate for nine years before sleep overtook him. When he awoke, he was so disappointed by his weakness that he tore off his eyelids and threw them to the ground so he would never nap again. From those bits of flesh grew the first tea trees.

When traders introduced tea to Europe in the sixteenth century, a global trade was born. Soon, Europeans clamoured for a cup of tea. In England, Queen Catherine of Braganza made taking tea a social event, and diarists recorded the excitement of this strange new drink. Importing tea all the way from China was an expensive business, so only wealthy people could afford to partake. The exorbitant price did little to diminish the desire for tea.

The cost added to a problem many European nations were facing, however. While Chinese products such as porcelain, silk and tea were in demand in Europe, there were no trade goods that the Chinese market would accept in return. The only way to pay for tea was to transport silver to China, and the flow of bullion out of Britain began to have a major effect on the economy. To help balance the trade, the British came up with an ingenious and nefarious scheme. In the nineteenth century, Britain had taken control of India, Afghanistan, and all of their opium poppies. While there was no desire for European goods in China, there was a growing market for the narcotic drug being intentionally fed by the British. China had banned opium in 1796, but within decades, British merchants were importing, illicitly, a thousand tonnes of the drug into the country. Addiction became rampant, and silver began to stream out of China to pay for it.

The Chinese cracked down on the trade in a number of ways, but this provoked the British into forcing open trade through military means. In 1839, the First Opium War broke out, which ended with the Chinese having to pay for opium supplies that they had destroyed and handing the island of Hong Kong to Britain. The treaty ending the war did not satisfy the British, as the Chinese still kept the importation of opium illegal. The Second Opium War of 1856 led to the legalization of opium and freedom of movement for British traders in China. The Chinese refer to the time that followed this as the Century of Humiliation.

Even a leaf falling into some water can create ripples that travel through time.

GOATS GET HIGH

The legendary origins of coffee also started with an accidental discovery – in this case, the failure to control some goats. The Ethiopian shepherd Kaldi is said to have noticed that his goats were nibbling on red berries and becoming unusually frisky. When Kaldi tried them himself, he was delighted with the caffeine high. Soon, Islamic scholars were using coffee to stimulate their studies.

XERXES INVADES GREECE AND LOSES SPECTACULARLY

· ·

Conquering Greece should have been the simplest of tasks for the Persian Empire in the fifth century BC. For a start, there was no single nation called Greece at the time. What we know as Greece was a mosaic of city states that spoke the same language but competed with each other for power and prestige and were rarely united.

By contrast, the Achaemenid Empire of Persia (550–330 BC) was one of the largest empires of its day. Stretching from Egypt to the Indus Valley, it contained a multitude of people who all owed allegiance to the *Shahanshah*, the King of Kings. An inscription of one Persian king lists twenty-nine kingdoms that belonged to him. The Great King, as the Greeks called Persia's ruler, could summon armies of unimaginable size and crush anyone who dared oppose him. Indeed, Persia had already conquered many Greeks who had founded cities on the coast of what is now Turkey.

The Persian king Darius had suffered a humiliating rebellion when these Greek cities rose against his rule, aided by other Greeks. After reconquering them, he turned his eyes to mainland Greece. Instead of a swift victory, his armies were conclusively beaten by the Athenians at the Battle of

Marathon. The first Persian invasion of Greece had been a debacle, but not every Persian gave up the dream of bringing the troublesome Greeks to heel.

Following Darius's death, his son and heir, Xerxes, became the Great King and prepared a vast army and navy to subjugate the Greeks. The mere threat of Persian force, plus the financial benefits of friendship with Persia, persuaded many city states to ally themselves with the invaders. In 480 BC, the Persian army marched into Europe. Our best, though not necessarily always reliable, source for the Persian invasion is the 'Father of History', Herodotus. He says that Xerxes led a force of 2.5 million men. Even if it was a more plausible two hundred thousand soldiers, then this was one of the largest armies ever assembled in the ancient world and must have seemed unstoppable.

Unfortunately, things went wrong rather quickly for the Great King. To cross into Europe, Xerxes ordered a bridge of boats to be constructed across the Hellespont for his men to march over. This was done, but almost immediately a storm struck, which broke the bridge and scattered the boats. In his fury, Herodotus tells us, Xerxes ordered that the waters of the Hellespont be punished by whipping them, plunging hot irons and iron manacles into the waves to show the Great King's mastery over the ocean. Those who had been in charge were beheaded. This seems to have encouraged their replacements to do a better job, and the army marched over a more solidly built bridge.

The Greeks, meanwhile, had ample time to prepare for the coming army. Those city states that had not already sided with the Persians formed an alliance to oppose them. Athens and Sparta, as the most powerful states, constituted the nucleus of resistance and were joined by dozens of other cities. It was decided that the advance of the Persian army should be blocked at the narrow pass of Thermopylae, while a Greek naval force at Artemisium would stop the Persian ships from bypassing the defenders.

The Battle of Thermopylae has become a symbol of defiance in the face of overwhelming force. Led by three hundred Spartans under their king Leonidas, the Greeks held off the numerically vastly superior Persian army for seven days. After a final three days of pitched battle, the Persians outflanked the Greeks via a mountain pass. Warned of the Persian manoeuvre, only the Spartan force and their Thespian allies remained to hold the pass, and they were massacred. Two of King Xerxes' brothers were slain. The Persian fleet at Artemesium did little better when storms wrecked hundreds of vessels. Having heard of the defeat at Thermopylae, the Greek ships pulled back to mount their defence elsewhere.

The Persian forces now essentially had free run of most

of Greece. The Greek defenders pulled back to the narrow isthmus of Corinth for a final stand. The citizens of Athens evacuated the city and sailed to the island of Salamis. It was at Salamis that the navy of Athens would face the might of Persia. The abandoned city of Athens was utterly sacked and destroyed by the Persian army.

At the Battle of Salamis, the Athenian commander Themistocles used trickery to hold the allied fleet together and divide the Persian navy. According to ancient sources, around four hundred Greek triremes faced one thousand two hundred Persian ships. In the narrow waters of the Straits of Salamis, the Persians were not able to outflank the Greeks. Xerxes, watching the battle from his throne on a clifftop, saw the defeat and scattering of his navy. It is not known how many Persian ships were lost, but the remainder retreated to safety while the Greeks dominated the seaways. Xerxes had not learned from the fiasco of his pontoon bridge across the Hellespont and attempted to cross over to Salamis in the same way. With Greek ships patrolling the waters, this was impossible.

Apparently fearing being cut off should the bridge over the Hellespont be severed again, Xerxes marched most of his forces back to his empire. His general, Mardonius, was left with a smaller army to finish the conquest of Greece, which Xerxes had already failed to do with a larger one. At the Battle of Plataea in 479 BC, the allied Greeks slaughtered the remaining Persian force, and Mardonius was killed. The Greeks had overcome the mightiest empire on Earth.

A DRAMATIC TRIUMPH

The Athenian playwright Aeschylus, who fought at the Battles of Marathon and Salamis, left one of the most memorable accounts of the Persian defeat in his play *The Persians*, first performed in 472 BC. Unsurprisingly, the Athenian crowd was thrilled by a retelling of their greatest victory and Aeschylus won first prize for drama that year.

Some historians say that the Greek account of Xerxes' invasion was overblown. Perhaps, they say, it was never meant to be a conquest, but merely a punitive expedition. Even if this were true, it was still a costly failure for Xerxes. Not only did Persia waste resources on an immense scale and leave thousands dead in pointless battles, it did the worst thing a power can do – it created an emboldened enemy, aware that Persia was not invincible.

The Greeks remained a troublesome neighbour for the Persian Empire for decades to come, until the armies of Alexander the Great destroyed Persia in 330 BC.

ALEXANDER FAILS TO NAME AN HEIR AND CAUSES CIVIL WAR

In 323 BC, Alexander the Great lay dying in his bed in Babylon, at the centre of the empire he had built through bloody conquest in just a few years. Setting out from Macedon, he had quelled rebellious Greek cities, brought Egypt under his control, driven the Great King from Persia, and led his army into India. No empire in history had ever covered so much territory. But now, aged just thirty-two, the conqueror was facing his final battle – one he could not win – against mortality itself.

Alexander had never spared himself in fights and was injured grievously multiple times during his campaigns. These wounds likely weakened him, and when he was struck down with an illness that caused chills, sweating and exhaustion, it became obvious that the king did not have long to live. This presented the men around him with a problem. A great king needs an heir or there will be chaos in the wake of his death, but Alexander had no legitimate children. His wife Roxana was pregnant at the time, but a foetus cannot wear a crown.

According to accounts of Alexander's deathbed, his greatest friends and generals were gathered around him and asked who should succeed him. Alexander simply replied, 'The strongest.' Unfortunately, many of the men who had followed Alexander to the edges of the known world considered themselves to be the strongest and therefore best suited to taking over the empire. It was even rumoured that one of them had hurried the death of Alexander with poison. Wars would soon be fought as each tried to claim the crown for themselves.

While Alexander is best known today for carving out his empire through warfare, another project of his might have been one of his most lasting legacies, had he lived. Alexander had no wish to rule over his domains as a conqueror. He wanted to forge his disparate conquests into a single multi-ethnic and multicultural kingdom where the cultures of East and West were unified.

Emblematic of his attempts to do so was the mass marriage he carried out in the Persian city of Susa between his chief officers and noble Persian women. Alexander had used diplomatic marriages to cement his own position by wedding high-born ladies after conquering their lands. His wife, Roxana, was a princess from Central Asia. Uniting

Greece and Persia by the marriage beds of his men, and not merely by their swords, was supposed to create children who could lay claim to the greatness of both civilizations.

There was resistance to this harmonization effort. Some of his men looked askance at their king garbed in the eastern fashions of the Persian Empire and took against appointing Persians to positions of power. Alexander also took to using forms and rituals that his new subjects would be familiar with, to secure their devotion. The most inflammatory of these was *proskynesis*, where people lay on the ground and kissed the earth when approaching the king. In Greek and Macedonian culture this was only performed before the images of gods, but in Persia it was the standard abasement when people presented themselves before the king.

What Alexander really needed was time, because people tend to resist change if it is forced on them too rapidly. For Greeks and Macedonians who cherished the ideal of liberty and had a long history of deriding the Persians as effete and barbaric, the merging of their civilizations had to be carried out gently. Alexander was in a rush with everything he did – one does not conquer the largest empire in the world tentatively. It was time that Alexander needed to fulfil his hopes of a unified empire, but it was time that was denied him when he breathed his last.

Those same men who had been Alexander's closest

friends in youth and had accompanied him on campaigns became, when he died, squabbling rivals ready to tear apart his empire to grasp their own fragment of it. None of them shared Alexander's dreams of creating a new empire where all, be they Greek, Persian, or Indian, were equal members.

The successors of Alexander, known as the Diadochi, abandoned the foreign wives that Alexander had forced on them. The only thing they dreamed of was power. Each sought to claim legitimacy for their rule over a portion of Alexander's conquests. Craterus rushed to Macedonia to have control of Alexander's remaining family, while Ptolemy literally stole the body of Alexander as it was on its way home to be buried, so that he could entomb it in his domain in Egypt. The new rulers soon declared themselves to be kings who, instead of uniting, constantly strove to wrest more land from their rivals. Only the strongest survived for long, as Alexander had predicted.

The Hellenistic period, as the time after the death of Alexander is known, did see a diffusion of Greek culture heavily influenced by its new surroundings. In Egypt, the Ptolemaic kings, who descended from Alexander's general Ptolemy, were worshipped as pharaohs in the traditional style, but also encouraged Greek learning in the Great Library of Alexandria. Hellenistic artistic styles spread into India. An engraved edict by the Indian ruler Ashoka, dating from the third century in Afghanistan, is written in Greek and Aramaic.

The synthesis of cultures in the wake of Alexander's life created new modes of living across Europe and Asia. Yet his death without an effective heir must be considered a missed opportunity in world history. Who knows what sort of culture might have arisen from a single powerful empire that could draw on influences from such a wide variety of peoples. No doubt, Alexander would have added even more nations to his dominion. At the very least, the costly wars of the Diadochi might have been avoided, which brought such bloodshed in the years after Alexander died.

A DEADLY INHERITANCE

Alexander's wife Roxana gave birth to a boy who became King Alexander IV, nominally the ruler of his father's empire. When Alexander reached the age of manhood, Cassander, regent of Macedon, had Alexander and Roxana poisoned and himself declared King of Macedon.

Hannibal Misses his Chance to Destroy Rome

· ·

The Punic Wars between Rome and Carthage raged in fits and starts from 264 to 146 BC. These two pseudo-democracies fought for dominance over the Mediterranean Sea, which the Romans would later simply call *Mare Nostrum* – Our Sea.

In the third century BC, the Roman state was aggressively expanding and came to control all of the Italian peninsula south of the Arno River. Carthage, in modern Tunisia, was a trading and maritime power that claimed coastal regions across North Africa, southern Spain and the islands of the Mediterranean. Its territory in Sicily brought Carthaginian forces within sight of the Roman mainland and sparked the first war. Carthage lost and was saddled with a vast set of reparations.

The Carthaginians could not pay this indemnity and were forced to look for ways to raise the tons of silver the Romans demanded. Spain was known to be rich in precious metals, so it was decided to expand their territories there and start mining operations. The man placed in charge of this was Hamilcar Barca, a hero of the war who nurtured a hatred for the Romans. With him he took his young son Hannibal, who was forced to swear an oath that he would never be a friend to Rome. He never was.

While aged just twenty-six years old, Hannibal took charge of Carthage's army in Spain and waited for a provocation, which would give him a reason to revenge himself on Rome. When the Romans laid claim to a town within Carthage's territory, he knew his time had come. The Second Punic War began.

Hannibal decided to strike at the heart of Rome, so he marched his army towards Italy and, famously, also took thirty-seven war elephants with him. His force suffered as they took the long journey through Gaul and over the Alps, battling Celtic tribes along the way, but the crossing of the Alps is one of the most remarkable achievements in military history. Despite losing thousands of men and animals to the harsh conditions of the trek, Hannibal arrived in the Po valley with a formidable army ready to take the fight directly to the Romans.

The Romans did not panic at the Punic foe arriving on their doorstep, however. They had recently conquered many of the tribes of Northern Italy, so they were used to fighting in that terrain. Their confidence was quickly tested when, at the Battle of Ticinus in 218 BC, a Roman army under Consul Publius Scipio was routed by Hannibal's cavalry, with heavy losses. A month later, Roman reinforcements arrived and met Hannibal at the battle of Trebia. The Romans were lured out of their camp and into a pitched battle, where the far superior Numidian cavalry swept the Roman horsemen from the field. Using clever tactics, the Roman infantry was enveloped and forced into retreat, but maybe twenty thousand Romans were left dead beside the River Trebia.

Bitter Roman death tolls became the pattern of Hannibal's invasion. At the Battle of Lake Trasimene, a Roman army was surprised by Hannibal as they marched beside the lake. The Romans were surrounded and pushed into the waters, where they either drowned under the weight of their armour or were cut down. Twenty-five thousand men died. The Romans were nothing if not determined, though; another army was raised and sent to crush Hannibal. Roman tactics at this time tended towards strict formations of men marching directly at enemy lines, to kill and scatter anyone who dared oppose them. The genius of Hannibal was to use this against them: armies kept coming, and he kept defeating them. With every victory, more Celtic tribes allied with Hannibal and even the Latin allies of Rome in the south began to turn against Rome, as they sensed the shifting tide.

The Battle of Cannae saw the apotheosis of Hannibal as one of history's greatest generals. In other battles, such as at Lake Trasimene, he had turned the terrain against his opponent or used other advantages to defeat the Romans. At the Battle of Cannae in 216 BC, the largest Roman army mustered until this point, over eighty thousand strong, faced the numerically weaker Carthaginians on an open plain. There would be no hidden forces emerging from woods or ravines – this was a straight fight to the death.

Again, Hannibal annihilated the Romans. Placing his weakest forces in the centre of his lines, he met the Romans in battle. As expected, the centre of Hannibal's army began to fall back, Romans poured into the space they left, and soon the Roman army was massing towards the centre, where there was least resistance. That is when the Carthaginian cavalry swung the trap and slammed into the rear of the Romans in a flanking manoeuvre that is still studied in military academies to this day. The Romans found themselves surrounded, packed together so tightly that many men were unable to raise their swords or shields to defend themselves. The rest of the day was slaughter, as the whole Roman force was put to death.

This was the moment. This was when Hannibal could have attacked the city of Rome itself. According to the Roman writer Livy, the cavalry commander, Maharbal, came to Hannibal and prophesied that if they marched immediately, then within five days they could be standing on the Capitol in Rome as the complete masters of Italy. Hannibal said that he needed time to draw up his plans. Maharbal is recorded to have said, 'The gods do not give all their gifts to one man. You know how to gain a victory, but you do not know how to use it.'

Perhaps Hannibal expected that this time, surely, the Romans would be forced to surrender to him. No country could continue to endure losses in which so many of their young men ended up as corpses, while their allies daily abandoned them. Hannibal may have hated the Romans, but he did not understand them. They would fight on.

The Romans did continue to raise forces and send them

against Hannibal. Hannibal often won, but he never again had the opportunity to assault the walls of Rome itself. It took the Romans sending an army to Carthage in 204 BC for Hannibal to finally leave Italy and defend his homeland.

RUNNING FROM THE ROMANS

After the Second Punic War, Hannibal fled before the Romans could demand his surrender. He moved from city to city, ever eastward, to avoid being captured, until he was welcomed at Ephesus by King Antiochus. When Antiochus was also defeated by the Romans, Hannibal once again fled. He met his end in Bithynia, where some said he took poison to ensure the Romans would never catch him.

We can never know whether Hannibal, who had won such outrageous victories, could have breached the walls of Rome and destroyed his enemy, but his not laying siege to the city must rank as one of the worst missed opportunities in the history of warfare. The end of the Second Punic War came on Carthaginian territory, not Italian, when Hannibal's forces were scattered at the Battle of Zama in 202 BC. A peace treaty was drawn up that saw Carthage stripped of much of its territory and demands made for the vast sum of ten thousand silver talents.

Even these punitive measures were not enough for Rome. The Third Punic War occurred in the 140s BC and ended with Carthage being utterly destroyed, hundreds of thousands killed and the rest of its population sold into slavery. Never again would Romans have to fear the dread news that *Hannibal ad portas* – Hannibal is at the gates.

Assassins Leave Mark Antony Alive – and Suffer his Vengeance

The Roman Republic was a writhing nest of politicians from great families, struggling for supremacy within the rule of laws designed to stop any one person from becoming too powerful. The chief magistrates, the consuls, were elected in pairs so that neither wielded total control, and they served for only a single year. Elections were fiercely fought, alliances were created and broken, and they were repeated year after year, with different figures rising and falling. The wheel of fortune that had turned the fates of Roman statesmen for centuries was broken in the first century BC by the supremacy of the Caesars.

Roman politics could very easily turn bloody when factions formed and fought for control. Civil wars had seen generals marching their armies into Rome, driving out their opponents, and posting proscription lists. Those named on these lists were marked for death, and those who killed them could claim a huge reward in gold. One person who got an early lesson in the fatal rewards of losing was Julius Caesar, who was named in the proscriptions. Caesar managed to escape death but learned that politics was a life-or-death game.

It is impossible to chart all of the steps in Caesar's rise to power here, but they involved making deals with other statesmen, conquering Gaul, and marching on Rome, in an echo of the earlier civil wars. Caesar was appointed dictator with broad powers to reorganize the government, including appointing magistrates as he saw fit. His most loyal supporters profited greatly from Caesar's largesse, including Mark Antony, a dissolute and impoverished nobleman but a skilled army commander. Antony was made governor of Italy as Caesar departed to the east, to finish off the forces of the Senate that opposed him.

At the battle of Pharsalus, the senate forces under Pompey the Great were defeated. Some senators fled to continue the civil war elsewhere, but many, such as Cicero and Marcus Junius Brutus, presented themselves to the victorious Caesar in hopes of a pardon. This was granted; with the final triumph of Caesar, many who had opposed him found themselves alive only because of his clemency. Few could forget that they owed him their lives, or that he held the reins of the state, which had once been in the grip of the Senate.

Caesar wallowed in the awards showered on him by a compliant Senate. He was made perpetual dictator, granted the right to sit on a golden chair during meetings of the Senate, and his face was the first of a living person ever to be struck on Roman coins. The days of the year itself belonged to him, as the month of Quintilius was renamed Julius in his honour. It seemed as if Rome was slipping towards monarchy. The hated, possibly legendary, kings of early Roman history had been cast from the city, and the entire Republican system was meant to stop anyone proclaiming themselves to be a king. Without uttering the word, Caesar was assuming the position.

Lucius Junius Brutus is supposed to have been the man who kicked out Lucius Tarquinius Superbus, the last King of Rome, in the sixth century BC. As one of the first consuls, he was held up as a hero of the Republic, and it was from him that Marcus Brutus, friend-turned-enemy of Caesar, claimed descent. When a conspiracy of senators was formed by Cassius in 44 BC to remove Caesar from power, Brutus was included in their number and came to be the leader of the movement.

The conspirators, or liberators, as they preferred to think of themselves, numbered among themselves those who had been personally wronged by Caesar, those who were jealous of his pre-eminent position, and those who genuinely loathed the idea of tyranny. Around sixty men were recruited, and the plans to pull Caesar down by assassination were made.

No dictator rules alone, and discussion turned to whether Caesar's allies should be killed as well. Most of the conspirators agreed that Mark Antony, who was consul that year, should die, as he was one of Caesar's closest associates and a man who could call on the loyalty of the legions. They feared that killing Caesar would just create the opportunity for Antony to take the vacant throne. Only Brutus spoke out against this. Plutarch records that Brutus believed that only the tyrant should be slain, perhaps to show that their motives were purely patriotic and not born out of revenge. Antony's life was saved, but history would judge if this was a wise act of clemency or not.

On the Ides of March, the conspirators struck during a meeting of the Senate, plunging daggers into the dictator and inflicting twenty-three bloody wounds. According to tradition, Caesar bled to death at the feet of a statue of his rival, Pompey the Great. Marcus Brutus stepped forward to address the senators and declare their new liberty, but, in a panic, the other senators pushed and shoved each other to flee the scene of the murder. The conspirators then moved to the streets to tell the people of Rome that they had been delivered from tyranny. Sullen crowds met them in silence.

Mark Antony, not knowing that he was not also facing death, fled the city in disguise, but returned once it became clear that the conspirators were not gaining the support of the Roman populace. Caesar had instituted populist reforms, while the conspirators all came from the aristocratic faction and had never courted the love of the plebs. Troops loyal to Caesar and Antony marched on the city to put down disorder. Even at the time, some considered sparing Antony to be a mistake. Cicero, who had been excluded from the conspiracy, wrote to one of them that if he had been involved, then Antony would have died.

At first, Antony seemed to defy most of the conspirators' fears, as he brokered a compromise with them to secure peace. This did not last. Antony began to condemn the conspirators not only as assassins but as parricides, because they killed the father of the nation. The conspirators left Italy to seek safety in the provinces, but this did not help them. Antony formed an alliance with Caesar's heir, Octavian, and it was decided that the conspirators had to be put to death.

Brutus and Cassius raised an army in the east to counter

Antony and Octavian's forces. It met at the battle of Philippi in Northern Greece, where the conspirators lost. Cassius and Brutus killed themselves to prevent falling into their enemies' hands. It is said that Antony covered Brutus's corpse in a purple cloak as a mark of thanks for having spared him during the assassination.

HOW NOT TO SURVIVE AN ASSASSINATION

While history does not record the names of all of the conspirators, those we do know mostly came to sticky ends. Some died by their own hands with Brutus and Cassius at Philippi, though Labeo required the help of a slave to drive a sword through his throat. Others were tortured to death. The last conspirator to die was Gaius Cassius Parmensis, who had managed to make peace with Antony. After Antony's defeat by Octavian, Parmensis retired to Athens – briefly, as he was soon beheaded by one of Octavian's men.

Any chance of a restoration of the Roman Republic died that day. It may be that attempting to govern such a large empire with the tools of the republican state was an impossible task, but once the conspirators were vanquished, there was nothing to stop the slide towards the imperial rule of emperors.

THE ROMANS LOSE AT THE TEUTOBURG FOREST

Virgil's epic poem the *Aeneid* describes the mythic history of the city of Rome, beginning with a group of exiles fleeing the siege of Troy and travelling to Italy in hopes of finding a new home. According to the poet, the gods meet to discuss what will happen to the race that will spring from the Trojans. Jupiter, king of the gods, reveals that he has granted the Romans the imperium sine fine – an empire without end.

When Virgil wrote these words in the second half of the first century BC, it must have truly seemed that there was no limit to how far the Romans would push their burgeoning empire. From a single city, the Romans had conquered lands as disparate as Spain, Egypt and Syria. Julius Caesar had even launched an invasion of Britannia in 55 BC, making it seem as if even the Great Ocean that encircled the world could not hold the Romans in.

Publius Quinctilius Varus (46 BC–AD 9) might have been

one of the most successful names to emerge from Rome during the era of Caesar's successor, Augustus. Varus's rise came from tying himself closely to the man who became Rome's first emperor. Aside from having an ancient and patrician name, he did not have much else to boast about before he allied himself to Augustus by making advantageous marriages that brought him close to Augustus's family. Apparently, marrying well was another path to empire without end, and this helped get him appointed to important governorships. While he was quelling a revolt in Judaea, we are told that Varus ordered the crucifixion of two thousand rebels. The ability to pacify a difficult region may have led to Varus's next appointment.

For several years, the Romans had been troubled by the tribes of Germania, who had the unfortunate tendency to raid into Roman Gaul. In 17 BC, members of the tribes had captured and executed several Romans, so a force under the general Lollius was sent to attack the Germans, but suffered a humiliating defeat and lost the eagle standard that was the symbol of Roman power. A number of eager generals had been sent in the aftermath to push the Roman frontier all the way to the Elbe River, which brought many obstreperous Germani under the sway of Rome – at least for a time.

Augustus considered the situation in Germany to be settled enough to organize the new territory into a province of the empire. It was now necessary to appoint officials to administer the province and begin the process of showing the inhabitants the benefits of Roman government. The man chosen as governor of Germania was none other than Publius Quinctilius Varus.

Varus is also said to have liked to use his governorships to enrich himself, though this would not have been that unusual in the Roman Empire. We are told that Varus entered the province as if the Germans only needed to taste the sweetness of Roman rule to be tamed. Then the cash would begin flowing. Varus did not see the need to act as a military general there, but the German tribes had other ideas.

The Romans had done their best to inculcate an appreciation for Roman civilization by befriending leaders of the German tribes. Arminius, son of the chief of the Cherusci tribe, had served with the Roman army, learned Latin and been granted Roman citizenship. It was hoped that German nobles who had received the hospitality of Rome would one day grow up to be useful allies. What Arminius, known to history as Herman the German, learned about how Roman armies functioned would indeed be useful, but not to Rome. He began to form an alliance of the tribes to bring down Varus and cast the Romans out.

In AD 9, Arminius convinced Varus that there was a

dangerous rebellion afoot and lured him into journeying deep into German territory. Varus took an army of over twenty thousand men and set out to put down the uprising. Though the true conspiracy against the Romans was revealed, Varus chose to ignore the intelligence and continue to trust Arminius. Weeks of marching without a military engagement may have made Varus eager for battle; at any rate, when Arminius suggested a route towards the enemy, Varus took it. Arminius left the Romans and took his men with him, he said, to raise the rest of his tribe to help in the coming battle.

The Roman army was moving through the densely wooded ground of the Teutoburg forest. The weather was bad and the roads worse, so the Roman formation lengthened as the baggage carts became stuck in mud. The army was stretched out and unable to form a strong defensive stance when thousands of Germans emerged from the woods and rained javelins down on them. The tribesmen melted away before the Romans could counterattack. Varus realized the weakness of his position and ordered a fortified camp to be constructed. There he held a council of war and, despite the dangers of operating in darkness, ordered a night march to escape.

Arminius had planned for this eventuality and ordered ditches and walls to be constructed across the road, to block the Roman advance. The Romans found themselves confined to a narrow gap between the wood and a deep bog, unable to move forward, when the main body of the Germans attacked. The power of the Roman army lay in the strong formations they used in battle to demolish their foes, but here the Romans were disorganized and, within just a few hours, almost the entire force, three legions, was cut down. Varus is said to have seen the destruction of his army and fallen on his sword. For that, at least, the Romans considered him brave, even as they lamented his skills as a general. The many failures of Varus to listen to warnings and to misunderstand his role as governor of a new and dangerous province marked Roman history for centuries.

HERMAN THE GERMAN

Arminius did not die by a Roman sword. Instead, he was poisoned by other Germans, who feared he was setting himself up as king. In the nineteenth century, he was held up as a heroic example by those seeking German unification. Today, a statue of Herman, as Arminius came to be known, standing 25 m (82 ft) tall, with his sword held aloft, guards the Teutoburg Forest.

The Germans were not satisfied with simply annihilating one army: the uprising took hold, and nearly every fort east of the Rhine was overrun. The remaining legions on the frontier were able to set up defences that held the German tribes on their side of the Rhine; otherwise, the Germans might have attacked deep into the heart of Gaul.

The loss of the battle in the Teutoburg forest has perhaps been credited with having too much of an impact on Rome's expansion into Germany. In all likelihood, there was nothing to gain from the direct government of Germany. What tax could be extracted from the Germans would not have covered the costs of garrisoning the province. The failure of Varus's forces, however, was a sharp lesson to the Romans not to underestimate the 'barbarians' who preferred not to become subjects of the emperors.

Steam Power is Used for Toys, not Industry

Hero, or Heron, of Alexandria lived in the first century AD and may have been the greatest inventor of his age. Little of his work survives, but, from what we do know, he created extraordinary objects that must have astounded those around him.

The people of Alexandria could have seen Hero's inventions everywhere, from the theatre to temples to musical displays. It was Hero who created the first vending machine, when he designed a way of dispensing holy water. The supplicant would place a coin into a slot on the top of the machine, which depressed a lever that released a set amount of blessed water. Even in these ancient times, money and religion were hard to disentangle.

At the theatre, punters could enjoy a ten-minute production that was entirely mechanical in nature. Through the use of pulleys, weights and rotating cogs, the action of the performance was set in motion. Both the humanoid automata and the scenery of the theatre moved. The machinery may even have been reprogrammable to offer different plays. Hero also invented a way of providing thunder for dramas by dropping balls onto a concealed drum.

While these machines were impressive, Hero also turned his practical mind to power and how it could be harnessed. Hero designed a musical organ that used wind to turn a wheel that drove a pump, which provided the air for the instrument. But the most intriguing of his inventions was the *aeolipile* – the world's first steam engine.

The *aeolipile* was a simple machine consisting of a hollow sphere with two siphons projecting in opposite directions. A reservoir of water was heated underneath the sphere, and the resulting steam was directed into it. From there, the steam emerged as pressurized jets that forced the sphere to spin rapidly. In this way, Hero demonstrated that heat could be easily converted into locomotion, yet the *aeolipile* was never used for practical or industrial purposes. Instead, it remained purely a scientific curiosity that was used to investigate the properties of pressure.

We know from his inventions that Hero understood the mechanics of moving objects. He had designed a temple door that opened when a fire was lit on an altar to drive the expansion of water. He also created a cart that was driven forward using ropes wrapped around the axles that were connected to a falling weight. Yet there is never any suggestion that he seriously considered the potential use of his *aeolipile* as a generator of force on a larger scale. Why he failed to consider this application remains unclear.

It may be that the technological limitations of his time made it impossible. Steam power, as used in the Industrial Revolution of the eighteenth and nineteenth centuries, relied on steel to create machines strong enough for the high pressures involved, as well as copious amounts of coal to heat them. Hero's device was made of copper, which could never have withstood the forces needed to create powerful engines. However, there may be another reason why the steam engines described by Hero in the first century remained simple curiosities.

Just as the modern world runs on oil, so the machinery of the Roman Empire was greased by the sweat of slaves. Wars of conquest brought in a constant stream of cheap human labour that was employed in every aspect of society, from mining to farming and teaching to administration. It was a poor Roman indeed who could not afford to buy at least one slave.

The philosopher Seneca told an anecdote about how the Senate once heard a motion to force slaves to wear some distinctive marker of their status, so they could be distinguished from citizens. The senators were aghast. If slaves could identify themselves by sight, they would soon realize just how many of them there were in the city and organize a revolt.

Many slaves were no doubt treated with respect by their masters, at least in the major Roman cities. Many were eventually set free and could earn a great deal of money as freedmen and women. In the countryside and in industry, however, slavery could be a brutal business indeed. Cato the Elder detailed how a good owner should treat their slaves: if they made a mistake, they should be beaten with a leather strap; if they committed a crime, they should be put to death in front of their fellow slaves, *pour encourager les autres*; and when a slave grew old or sick, they should be auctioned off as if they were a faulty piece of farm equipment. Even other Romans thought Cato's methods cold-blooded, but they probably reflected the reality of slavery in the empire.

With cheap and disposable labour in abundance, why would the Romans need to create technology to do their work for them? Anecdotes from the time show that even the Romans themselves recognized that technological advances could lead to unwanted unemployment. In Suetonius's *Life of Vespasian*, he tells the story of an engineer who came to the emperor and promised to move several heavy columns, by some unknown invention, up a hill in Rome for a lower price than even slaves could match. The emperor thought highly of this innovation and gave the engineer a valuable reward, but he refused to use his invention. 'You must allow the poor to earn their bread,' he supposedly said.

GOING DEEPER UNDERGROUND

By the seventeenth century, Europeans were coming to rely on coal for heat, instead of wood. The large amount of energy contained in coal made steam power feasible, but mining it was a dangerous and difficult business. The deep mineshafts would often flood. In 1698, Thomas Savery patented a pump powered by steam to pull water out of mines, but it had the unfortunate tendency of exploding. However, improved pumps powered by steam made ever-deeper mines possible, and allowed for more coal to be used in more steam engines.

Had the principles of Hero's steam engine been put to productive use, they would have created a revolution, and thousands of labourers would have been put out of work.

One can imagine that, if steam-powered machinery had been invented one thousand seven hundred years earlier, then the Luddites who targeted those machines would also have arisen equally prematurely.

The failure to make use of inventions such as Hero's for any serious purpose was a missed opportunity, but one that makes sense in context. Regardless, the idea of Romans riding steam engines to war is one that continues to fascinate counterfactual historians to this day.

ROMAN PERSECUTIONS FAIL TO SUPPRESS CHRISTIANITY

The Roman world was saturated with gods. The major gods Jupiter, Minerva, Mars and Vesta guarded Rome and were credited with controlling its fortunes. Before battles and wars, the gods were consulted, and offerings were made for their approval. There were also minor gods, who watched over the households of individual Romans and might be worshipped at a private shrine in the home. These represented everything from the concept of abundance to a goddess in charge of hinges.

In the early empire, the emperors and their families tended

to be deified upon their deaths. Vespasian even cracked a joke about this when, having realized he was dying, he said, 'Alas, I think I am becoming a god.' This practice started under Augustus, who had his adoptive father declared to be divine. Cynically minded people might say that this was just so he could describe himself as *divi filius* – the son of a god. Of course, someone else born during the reign of Augustus was described as the Son of God, and that was Jesus.

The Roman pantheon of gods was a flexible system, and many new gods were incorporated into it as the empire expanded, yet some gods were beyond the pale. The Christians, as the new sect born in the Near East came to be known, were not amenable to being co-opted. They declared that there was only one God, and refused to worship the traditional gods of Rome.

This created many troubles for early Christians, because religious worship in the ancient world had to be performed in public and for the good of the state. Those who refused to sacrifice to the gods and the emperors were refusing to do their part for the maintenance of Rome itself. They were traitors. The church fathers also took a dim view on everything from festivals to jewellery to military service as worldly distractions from contemplation on the divine. For pagan Romans, the Christians must have seemed like a dangerous and antisocial infection in the body politic.

Rumours soon spread that Christians carried out secret rituals in which they went so far as to consume the flesh and blood of a human in order to worship someone who had been a criminal and who died miserably on a cross.

Persecutions of Christians were common and widespread from the first to the fourth centuries. The first mention of public condemnation of Christians comes from Tacitus, who says that Nero claimed followers of a certain Chrestus were responsible for the Great Fire at Rome and had them punished. Our best source on how Christians were treated comes from the letters of Trajan and Pliny the Younger in the early second century.

Pliny, as governor of the province of Bithynia, was facing a tricky problem. He was being inundated with accusations against people believed to be Christians. What was he to do? Pliny tells his emperor that he has the accused interrogated several times and, if they persist in clinging to their Christianity, he executes them. Those who burned incense before an image of the emperor and cursed Christ, Pliny allowed to go free. Trajan wrote back, saying that Pliny was doing exactly the right thing, but he should not allow anonymous accusations to lead to investigations of suspected Christians. As long as Christians stayed quiet and hidden, they were mostly left alone.

Most 'persecutions' of Christians stayed on this low-level and local basis. Under Marcus Aurelius, executions of Christians occurred in Northern Africa and at Lyon in France, but much of the pressure for these actions seems to have come from local populations who resented the presence of Christians. In AD 250, however, the emperor Decius enacted an edict that led to the first empire-wide persecution of Christians, ordering everyone in the empire (except for Jews) to perform a public sacrifice to the gods in front of witnesses. We do not know how many Christians died for their refusal to offer sacrifice, but we do know that many apostatized and returned to the old religion, because several Christian sources describe difficulties in knowing whether such people could still be considered true Christians, having once returned to paganism. The reign of Diocletian, beginning in AD 284, marked the beginning of a great persecution, but it failed to check the rise of Christianity.

Instead of a policy of persecution and execution, removing Christians from the empire may have helped to spread the word of Christ and create new converts. Those that the Romans put to death as obstinate criminals were called martyrs by other Christians. Tales of the final days of these martyrs were one of the most popular forms of Christian text in the ancient world. By showing the martyrs as steadfast in their faith and displaying miraculous calm in the face of horrific torture, Christians could validate their new religion. Martyrs became the first saints of the church.

The more lurid the narrative of a saint's death, the more likely it was to be retold, and the more Christians could take heart in the righteousness of their faith. St Bartholomew is said to have been flayed alive, which is why statues of him often show the saint holding his own skin. St Agatha can be seen carrying her breasts on a platter after they were ripped off. Others were boiled to death, coated in scalding oil, or set on by wild dogs, and hagiographies of the saints' lives focused heavily on such excruciating ends.

The most famous persecution involves the throwing of Christians to wild animals. *Damnatio ad bestias* saw criminals of all sorts condemned to face beasts in the arena, fighting off anything from a wild boar to a lion, a bull to a hippopotamus, as the crowd roared their delight. Christian versions of such events like to say that, through prayer, many of the martyrs were able to, at least temporarily, quell the savage beasts.

There is no doubt that many Christians were put to death by the Romans, but most scholars now agree that the practice was nowhere near as widespread as the early Christian writers would have us believe. It does not matter. Early Christians believed it, and could probably point to local examples in which someone had been beheaded for refusing to abjure their faith. If a person they knew had been killed, was it really so absurd to think a faithful Christian woman somewhere hundreds of kilometres away had been fed to pigs? The real persecutions gave credence to fanciful tales. By seeking to suppress the Christians, the Romans had only created an army of martyrs, real or imagined, who could confront them in a way no flesh-and-blood army could combat. Words spread faster than swords.

In AD 306, the emperor Constantine came to the imperial throne and soon declared that the persecutions were at an end and that Christians could now worship freely in his empire. Christianity had not been vanquished by the execution of some of its members, but strengthened.

LAUGHING SAINTS

When St Lawrence was condemned to death, he was slowly roasted over a fire. This seems not to have depressed him, as he is alleged to have called out to his tormentors, 'You can turn me over now, this side is well done.' St Lawrence is the patron saint of comedians.

JULIAN INVADES PERSIA – IT GOES BADLY

In AD 331, Flavius Claudius Julianus, known to history as Julian, was born into the imperial family as a nephew of Constantine the Great. As a young man, he was brought up in the Christian faith and came of age during the reign of Constantine's sons. Though they were all Christians, they behaved with unchristian brutality towards their family. Uncles, cousins and other relatives were executed to ensure that the emperor's power was unquestioned. Julian was raised in an environment in which death could come at any time.

Julian and his brother were kept secluded from politics and placed in the care of Christian teachers and guardians. Despite this, Julian managed to accumulate a great deal of philosophical education, though he hid it under a veneer of orthodox piety. In fact, Julian's writings say that it was hearing his teachers attack the works of philosophers that first exposed him to their thoughts, and he sought out pagan wisdom when he was able. The times were still tumultuous, however, and two of the co-rulers of the empire died in civil wars until only Constantius II was left standing. His pruning of the imperial family meant that he had to turn to Julian and his brother as potential successors, because there was no one else left alive. Even so, Julian's brother was soon put to death for a perceived lack of loyalty, and Julian himself was held under close watch in case he also proved to be a traitor.

When Constantius II needed a leader in Gaul to ensure peace, he sent Julian with an army. Julian had never served in the military, yet, to the surprise of many, he turned out to be an able commander and governor. He led his army against the Germanic tribes, which were bedevilling the borders of the Roman Empire, and scattered the enemy. This won him the affection of his men, so that when, in AD 360, he was ordered to break up his army to aid Constantius II against a Persian invasion, the soldiers mutinied so as not to have to serve in this new war. They declared Julian to be the new emperor, and he soon led the army towards Constantinople to fight his cousin for power.

When Constantius II fell ill and died before his forces could face Julian's in battle, the empire passed peacefully into Julian's hands. He reformed its wasteful and inefficient government and modelled it on that of earlier emperors, such as Hadrian and Augustus. Julian threw off his pretence of Christianity and proclaimed that he would worship the old pagan gods of Rome. For this act, he is forever known to Christian historians as Julian the Apostate. To bolster the power of pagans, he forbade Christians to teach the ancient classics. Since this was the cornerstone of Roman education, it essentially removed all Christian professors from their roles. Temples were founded and reorganized, and the great oracles of Greece were resurrected. It looked as if Christianity would pass away as quickly as it had risen.

There seems to have been no widespread discontent against Julian's religious policy at the time, though Christian writers were understandably hostile towards him. Given enough time, who knows how far Julian might have succeeded in removing Christianity as a major power in the Roman Empire.

There was only one force at the time that might have driven Julian and his pagan reformation from their position. The throne of the Roman Empire rested on the backs of the common soldiers. More than once, a revolt by the soldiers had cast down one ruler and set up their own commander as a new one. Julian's army from Gaul could be relied on to support him, but the army manning the eastern borders might well have thought someone else would be a better monarch. To prove himself, the new emperor needed to win the loyalty of these forces. A successful military campaign and the bounties that would be handed out afterwards might be just the thing to bind those armies to him. The unrest on the eastern border gave Julian an excuse to invade the Persian Empire, and he set out to capture their capital at Ctesiphon.

With nearly a hundred thousand men, Julian crossed into

the Persian Empire, rebuffing all negotiated terms that the Persians offered. Towns and forts fell to the Romans as they marched down the Euphrates River towards their target. If the Romans could capture the Persian king, then they might swiftly complete a regime change and place a more amenable ruler in his place. Julian would be acclaimed as one of the greatest emperors in Roman history.

But things started to go wrong. The walls of Ctesiphon proved impregnable, and the Romans were left milling uselessly around the gates. It became obvious that laying siege to the city would be fruitless, as Persian forces would arrive to relieve the city long before it fell. Julian decided to march further into Persian territory to seek out more conquests, but this move left reinforcements he was expecting unable to reach him. His enemies scorched the earth ahead of the Roman army to deny it food, and flooded the land behind it to hinder a return. In the face of this situation, the decision was made to turn towards Roman territory, but along the way, the Romans were harried by their opponents.

In the Battle of Samarra, the army was caught on the march by an attack on the rear of their force. Julian launched into action by racing towards the fight with just his sword and some light armour. Julian managed to rally his men and lead a daring charge to force the Persians back. In the midst of the battle, Julian was cut off from his bodyguard, and, in the confusion, a cavalryman's spear grazed his arm and cut deep into his abdomen. Julian bravely tried to pull the spear out, but its sharp edges slashed his fingers open, and the emperor slipped from his horse. His guards recovered him, but the spearhead had punctured Julian's liver, and he died two days later. So, too, did the hopes of pagan Romans for the complete restoration of their faith.

THE PHILOSOPHER KING

Julian was not just interested in pagan theology; he also had an interest in Greek philosophy. He even cultivated the beard, which was the sign of a deep thinker. For this and other things, he was mocked by the citizens of Antioch. So Julian wrote a satire against them named *Misopogon* – Beard-Hater.

Christian historians leapt on the bloody death of the Apostate, after just two years of rule, as a welcome sign of divine judgement. Their accounts tell us that Julian saw the folly of his attempts to combat Christianity by having him say, with his dying breath, 'Thou hast conquered, O Galilean.'

Julian was the last pagan emperor of the Roman Empire. Just two decades after his attempts to bring back the old gods, the emperor Theodosius launched a persecution against pagans. In Rome, the fire of Vesta, the traditional hearth of the entire Roman world, was extinguished, never to be lit again. The Galileans had indeed won.

THE CHINESE FAIL TO FIND IMMORTALITY

Why do humans have to die? This is one of humanity's oldest philosophical questions. The Mesopotamian tales of Gilgamesh are among the most ancient stories that still survive, and at their heart is the quest for immortality. Though the hero Gilgamesh manages to find a herb that will grant him endless life, it is eaten by a snake before he can consume it. Eventually, Gilgamesh manages to make peace with the fact that he will eventually die – but his would not be the last quest for immortality.

Taoism was one of the major philosophical and religious schools in ancient China and is said to date back to the works of Lao Tzu at some point in the first millennium BC, though it seems to have grown out of various native beliefs.

Lao Tzu taught that the goal of humans should be to live in harmony with the Tao, which can be translated as 'the way', but as a concept encompasses the whole natural order and the underlying principles that govern the universe.

Many schools of Taoism developed over the centuries, pursuing various esoteric methods of achieving spiritual harmony and immortality. While Taoists believe in the immortality of the soul after death, they also thought it was no bad thing to extend the length of their lives. Some sought to channel the energies of the body through meditation, a process known as internal alchemy. If the body is thought of as a cauldron, then various aspects of thought, breath and rest could be added to brew an elixir of immortality within it.

Not everyone was able to achieve the calm necessary for internal alchemy, so they searched for an answer to death through external alchemy. Using rare ingredients, they tried to create a medicine that would indefinitely ward off death. The early practice of external alchemy was mainly interested in the proper way to perform rituals, but as objects, rocks and herbs were given specific meanings, practitioners started to craft their own recipes and procedures to achieve their ends.

Legends of immortality have a long history in China. The Peaches of Immortality, which grow only every six thousand years, were consumed by the wise immortals at special feasts. Images of peaches became common symbols of longevity in

Chinese art, but what about those who wanted to live forever without waiting for the Peaches of Immortality to ripen? For them, there was the Pill of Immortality.

The search for the Pill of Immortality reached its height in the second century AD. One possibly legendary alchemist, Wei Boyang, was said to have discovered how to make these pills, and used them to fly directly up to heaven. The exact recipe was not recorded, but alchemists of this time invented a number of highly technical processes for purifying the chemicals they used in their creations. The liquid metal mercury could be extracted from the mineral cinnabar, while 'true lead' was extracted from common lead ore. It should not escape notice that both lead and mercury can be highly injurious to human health.

There were many fatalities caused by the search for bodily eternal life. Over the course of Chinese history, scores of emperors and nobles were poisoned by the elixirs they consumed. Alchemists who worked with mercury vapour were known to experience strange visions that hinted at arcane powers, while in reality they were a side effect of mercury toxicity. The harsh and mercurial natures of several rulers have been attributed to mental instability caused by their consumption of various Pills of Immortality. The fifth-century AD emperor Daowu is supposed to have recognized the dangers of alchemical experimentation. His court alchemist was given prisoners on whom to test his creations before the emperor would allow the elixirs to pass his lips. The alchemists failed in their hunt for immortality, but they did stumble upon one successful formula for a very different substance.

The work of the alchemists led to many startling discoveries. Isolating chemicals gave the alchemists a large toolkit of ingredients to mix and see what emerged from their crucibles. No one can say exactly when a mixture of saltpetre, sulphur and a source of carbon was first mixed, but one ninth-century text warns against heating them together, as they could erupt into flames and smoke: gunpowder had been born.

At first, this explosive powder was probably used for purely medicinal purposes. Taking the power of gunpowder inside the body must have seemed like an efficient way of putting its energy to use. But the true power of gunpowder took some time to uncover. While the ingredients were common, the exact recipe has to be precisely calculated if it is to be truly explosive rather than just flammable and smoky.

Gunpowder was first used as a way of setting fire to buildings by coating arrows in it and igniting them before firing them at a target. It was a relatively short time before, instead of simply setting the arrows aflame, the gunpowder was used to drive the projectiles. Rockets using gunpowder as a propellent probably emerged in the thirteenth century. Bombs made from pots of gunpowder had already been used in sieges and battles. More exotic weapons were soon created that employed gunpowder's deadly effects. A fire lance was essentially a spear with a tube of gunpowder on the end, which could be jabbed at an enemy. Mixing small balls into the gunpowder would have made these weapons something like a blunderbuss, and must have terrified the first people they were used against.

DEADLY IMMORTALITY

The first emperor of a united China, Qin Shi Huang of the third century BC, is said to have expended a great deal of time and effort on discovering an elixir of immortality. This harmed both himself and others. Those sent to find recipes to ward off death were sometimes killed when they failed; one explorer refused to return to China for fear of retribution. The emperor may have been driven mad by the mercury he consumed – his tomb is rumoured to be filled with lakes and rivers of the very mercury that killed him.

Europe got its first experiences of gunpowder in the thirteenth century but it remained a rare and terrifying novelty on the battlefield. At the Battle of Crécy in 1346, the English army was able to stun the French force with both stones fired from cannons and small lead bullets from more portable gunpowder weapons. The main fighting, though, was still carried out by archers, knights and men-at-arms with handheld steel weapons.

Once each soldier was armed with a gun, much of the training and personal heroics of the age of chivalry was swept away forever. War became a simple game of who could obliterate their foes most efficiently with a hail of bullets.

Once an invention with so much potential for martial use has been made, it is impossible to keep it contained. It spread across the globe and changed the nature of warfare forever. It's ironic that the search for immortality directly led to the deaths of millions.

Part II

THE MIDDLE AGES

THE NORSE ABANDON
NORTH AMERICA

. . . .

The Icelandic Sagas, probably written in the thirteenth and fourteenth centuries, represent one of the most thrilling bodies of literature in world history. They record the family histories of the Norse as they settled on Iceland and abound with heroes, villains, crafty tricks and epic battles. The sagas are populated by characters who exult under names such as Thorfinn Skull-Splitter and Eystein Foul-Fart.

The adventures recorded by the sagas can seem far-fetched, but scholars agree that they offer insights into Norse society and history in the years before the conversion to Christianity. Much that is recorded in the sagas can never be verified, but for some there has been confirmation through archaeological discovery.

The Sagas of Eirik the Red and the Greenlanders tell us the strange story of how the Norse came to inhabit, or at least visit, the North American continent centuries before Columbus crossed the Atlantic. It begins, as many sagas do, with a cycle of bloodshed and revenge. Eirik's slaves are killed after causing a landslide that devastates a neighbouring farm on Iceland, provoking a round of killings and retribution that ends with Eirik fleeing to a new landmass to the north-west he had heard rumour of. What Eirik finds is a bitter land of ice and rock, but to encourage others to join his new colony, he names it Greenland, to suggest it is abounding with fertility.

It was from Greenland that the Norse apparently first discovered North America, though two different accounts exist. Both attribute it to a failure to keep a ship on course for the Greenland colonies. In one version, it is Leif the Lucky who is blown astray by a storm and stumbles on a land filled with grain, vines and trees. The Saga of the Greenlanders credits the discovery to Bjarni Herjolfsson, who is sailing for Greenland when he becomes lost in fog. When the mists lift, he spots rich and green vistas, but, despite Eirik's propaganda, he knows this is not what Greenland is like, so he sails away with news of his discovery.

The colonists are then said to have set out to populate these mysterious but tempting new shores, which must at least have presented an easier prospect than the harsh, icy winters of Greenland. The sagas are filled with weird happenings, ghosts and divine actions. The colonists face perils from poisonous whale meat and tempestuous seas, but they also uncover a wealth of natural resources. Islands are watered by fresh streams, there are nesting sites filled with tame birds where their eggs carpet the ground and sweet grapes are everywhere for picking. They name the new territory Vinland, in honour of the vines.

But the Norse travellers face internal and external threats. Having left the old world did not mean they had left old rivalries behind. Disputes spiral and lead to violence. When Freydís quarrels with a pair of brothers during one expedition, she stirs up her own men to slay them and their retainers. When her followers refuse to slay the women present, Freydís herself calls for an axe and slaughters them.

Perhaps the most interesting aspect of the sagas is the anthropological insights they give into the native inhabitants of North America at this time. The Norse tales call the locals Skrælings, and first contact between them and the Europeans is not peaceful. In the first meeting, eight of the native Americans are killed. That night, innumerable hide-boats carrying Skrælings appear and attack the Norse camp. One of the Norse leaders is pierced by an arrow and dies from his wounds. While there is eventually some trade between the Norse and the native peoples, misunderstandings always threaten the peace. An angry bull spooks native traders and sparks a battle that leaves many dead.

The sagas end with the Norse settlers returning to Greenland after various lengths of time in North America. The winters were still hard in the northern locations they visited, and people often died of hunger or sickness. The longest-lasting Norse colony in North America only survived three years before being abandoned, and the settlers returned to their old homes. After these abortive attempts at colonization, the Norse never attempted to stay in North America again.

Though these sagas were well known to historians, few took the stories of Norse settlements in North America seriously. Perhaps they were simply another invention, given that the sagas regale listeners with one-legged humanoids and other fantastical elements. However, Helge and Anne Stine Ingstad were convinced the sagas contained a nugget of reality. In 1960, they were scouring Newfoundland in

Canada for evidence of Norse habitation and, at L'Anse aux Meadows, found it.

Ruins that resembled the farms of Norse Greenland were excavated, and indisputable evidence of Norse habitation sprang from the ground, including jewellery, spinning tools and iron nails. Dating has placed the construction of the buildings here at around AD 1021. Most historians agree that L'Anse aux Meadows served as the base for the Norse, which allowed them to explore further south on the North American continent.

Ever since this discovery, people have wondered how and why the Norse did not expand into North America. Some even dream of a globe-spanning Norse world that could have been. The failure of the Norse colonies, though, was almost certain from the moment they stumbled into the New World.

The Norse were indeed spread across much of Europe, and along rivers deep into Russia. They traded and raided far and wide, using their superbly engineered boats and navigational skills. But it was probably trade that doomed the Norse colonies. Though they found timber and food, the colonies were not the land of milk and honey portrayed in the sagas. Famine struck them repeatedly, and they would have needed to regularly import many of the farm animals they relied on.

The distances to North America, even with stops in Iceland and Greenland, made trade between the new colonies and Europe both expensive and difficult. What did the colonies have to offer the old world that would make it worth sustaining a presence there? There was no easily mined gold or iron. Greenland only remained inhabited by the Norse as long as the walrus ivory they hunted for was in demand in Europe. As soon as tastes changed and the ivory was no longer valuable, Greenland was abandoned. The colonies in North America had little to offer and required heavy support.

WELL-TRAVELLED WOMEN

The sagas paint a vivid picture of the Norse women who join their husbands on journeys to the west. Gudrid and her husband, Thorfinn Karlsefni, led one of the expeditions. There, Gudrid gives birth to a son, the first European born in the Americas, whom they name Snorri. After returning to Iceland, Gudrid converts to Christianity and embarks on a pilgrimage to Rome, making her one of the most well-travelled people of her age.

There was also the matter of the native peoples who already lived in the lands the Norse were seeking to colonize. Though they lacked their iron weapons, they far outnumbered any Norse in North America. The Norse were not known for their docility, so conflict was almost inevitable and would only have ended one way.

THE WHITE SHIP SINKS, LEADING TO CIVIL WAR

Following the conquest by William the Conqueror in 1066, the monarchs of England found themselves in possession of a split kingdom. Their ancestral lands were across the Channel in Northern France, but England was the largest of their domains. Matters were further complicated by the fact that the Duchy of Normandy, the Norman homeland, was held by them through fealty to the French Crown. This led to no end of meddling, as French kings sought to humble the upstart British kings by interfering with how they governed Normandy.

The English kings of the medieval period would often have to cross the seas that separated their lands, either to fight for their rights or to pay homage to Paris. In the days of sail-powered wooden vessels, this trip was not a trivial endeavour. Ships could be delayed for days or weeks should the wind be against them, and there was always the possibility of being wrecked in a storm. Kings may be powerful, but they cannot control the weather.

Henry I of England was the son of the Conqueror and had reached the throne after the suspicious death of his older brother, William II, in a hunting accident. When his elder brother Robert Curthose, who had become Duke of Normandy, stirred up trouble, Henry I invaded and took Normandy under his personal guardianship in 1106. Robert Curthose was imprisoned, and King Henry thought his own son, William Adelin, should become the Duke, while the French king wanted Robert Curthose's son to inherit the Duchy. Henry I visited Normandy several times to support his son. In 1116, a rebellion broke out there that needed to be quelled.

In 1120, after years of conflict and political wrangling, Henry I emerged victorious. Normandy was given to his son William Adelin, in an arrangement agreed upon by the French king. All that remained was for the English royal court to return to England to celebrate their success. Some, however, began celebrating a little early.

Henry I set sail from Barfleur in France. He had been offered for the voyage the services of the *Blanche-Nef*, the

White Ship, which was thought to be swift and luxurious. Having already planned his journey, the king turned this down, but he did allow his son William Adelin, and others of the court, to travel on the White Ship. As young, privileged people who have just been granted vast tracts of land are wont to do, William Adelin and his companions became uproariously drunk. They did not keep their drinks to themselves but generously – and disastrously – handed out alcohol to the sailors.

At some point, the young people came up with a brilliant wheeze. Though the king's ship had left earlier, wouldn't it be great if the White Ship managed to arrive before him? Everyone agreed this would be a fantastic achievement, so all the sails were put out and the oars pulled with great vigour. The White Ship is said to have departed the harbour as swiftly as an arrow. It must have seemed like a grand adventure. There were no obvious perils on the horizon, and the weather was fair and clear. Within minutes, however, it had all gone wrong, and the hopes of Henry I for his succession were wrecked and scattered.

The White Ship struck a submerged rock and immediately began to sink beneath the waves. The prince's companions must have sobered up quickly, for they pushed William Adelin into a small boat and began to row him away from the disaster. One chronicler tells us that William Adelin might have survived the wreck, but on hearing one of his illegitimate sisters calling out for help, he ordered the boat to turn around and rescue her. The sea was full of struggling and desperate people, and as they tried to haul their way onto the little boat, it was swamped and sank. William Adelin, heir to England and aged just seventeen, disappeared beneath the churning sea.

Of the three hundred people packed onto the White Ship, only one is said to have survived the wreck: Burold, described as a 'rustic', who had just witnessed the extinction of the flower of English nobility. Onboard alongside William Adelin were two of King Henry I's illegitimate children, earls, lords, sons of lords and important members of the king's household, all of whom died.

In the aftermath of the disaster, the king was kept unaware of what had befallen his son. The lords are said to have all wept bitterly for their drowned relatives, but they were all too afraid to tell Henry I that his heir was gone. Eventually, a young boy was sent to the king with the news. When Henry heard that his sole legitimate son had been lost, he collapsed under the weight of the disaster.

It is little wonder that Henry was crushed. The carefully won peace in France was dependent on a marriage alliance that William Adelin was to make. What had been a triumph crumbled as quickly as the hull of the White Ship. It also threw the succession of the English throne into doubt, as although Henry had sired an impressive number of illegitimate children with his mistresses, he had only two legitimate children with his wives: William Adelin and Matilda. Matilda had been married to the Holy Roman Emperor, and it was to her that the king now turned.

We think of inheritance as an easy thing for monarchs because, under primogeniture, the crown passes to the oldest surviving sons and then daughters. But this was not the case in England at this time. When William the Conqueror had died, the crown of England went to his second son, William Rufus, while his oldest son had inherited Normandy. It was often left to the children of kings to fight for what they got. Henry I decided to force his nobles to accept Matilda as their queen when he died, by extracting oaths for their support.

A TOILET BREAK SAVES A LIFE

Stephen of Blois had been aboard the White Ship before it set sail. Accounts of how he came to leave the ship differ. Some say he was already too drunk and had to disembark. Others say that he was suffering from diarrhoea and so could not face a sea voyage. His decision not to sail changed the course of English history.

When Henry I died in 1135, the barons, if they had honoured their pledges, should have proclaimed Matilda as their new queen. But Matilda was in France at the time, and Henry's nephew, Stephen of Blois, a well-liked and capable man able to call on huge amounts of money, travelled quickly to London, where he convinced both the nobility and the people that he would make the better monarch. The Church also supported Stephen, and crowned him king.

The decades that followed are known in English history as the Anarchy, as armies marched across the land in support of either Matilda's or Stephen's claim. Only the accession of Henry II, Matilda's son, after Stephen's death in 1153, brought an end to the fighting.

ERFURT LATRINE DISASTER

. . . .

Few historians like to delve too deeply into toilets. How humans get rid of their waste has been somewhat overlooked as a driver of history. This is understandable, as evolution has bred us to have a disgust for faecal issues that must have saved many lives over the millennia. When we smell something like a toilet we recoil, so we are less likely to become contaminated by waste that may be harbouring infectious diseases.

The development of sewage systems and toilets that carry faeces away to a safely distant place is among the most important hygienic advancements ever made. Examining how societies deal with their toilet waste provides valuable insights into their level of organization. It also often contains valuable information for historians.

We can, for example, trace the path of the Lewis and Clark expedition across North America in 1804–06, thanks to the high levels of mercury in their bowel evacuations due to them taking purgative pills known as Rush's Thunderclappers, which were high in the toxic element. Examination of toilet pits can reveal the diets of our ancestors and the parasites they were infested with. Also, people often drop things in the toilet, so many artefacts have been retrieved by archaeologists with a strong stomach and a sieve.

Humans are vulnerable to attack when caught in the middle of visiting the toilet. There were several assassinations of important people that reputedly took place on the toilet. Godfrey the Hunchback, Duke of Lorraine, was stabbed from beneath with a spear while reliving himself in 1076. Edmund II of England was also supposed to have died in 1016 from an assassin's blade stuck into his fundament, or possibly crossbow bolts shot upwards, wielded by a murderer waiting in the latrine.

Sometimes it is the toilets themselves that make history. Today, we tend to think we are safe when using the toilet, thanks to the robust construction of modern buildings, but they were once risky places to visit. In medieval buildings the toilet was simply a seat that projected from a wall, where your waste would drop into a pit or the street below. There must have been many accidents in which these collapsed and people tumbled to their deaths.

We do know that medieval buildings had a much higher tendency to fall down spontaneously. Records from Germany in the twelfth and thirteenth centuries frequently record the palaces of princes and bishops collapsing. Floors could and did crack and collapse, walls tumbled down and staircases shattered with alarming regularity. The risks of simply being inside must have added to the tension at difficult meetings during a crisis.

In late July 1184, the King of Germany, Henry VI, who was the son of the Holy Roman Emperor Frederick Barbarossa, had to call a gathering of his nobles together to settle a vexing dispute between two of his quarrelsome vassals. Informal meetings, known as *Hoftag* or imperial diets, were often called to decide border issues and political matters and could be held wherever the court happened to be. The Holy Roman Empire was a patchwork of often competing principalities in which each ruler nominally owed allegiance to the emperor but was not above stealing land from their neighbours. So it was that Henry VI held a diet at Erfurt to resolve a contentious border issue between Mainz and Thuringia that was threatening to erupt into open war.

Louis III, Landgrave of Thuringia and a nephew of the

emperor, was in dispute with Conrad, the Prince-Archbishop of Mainz. Conrad had constructed a castle on the border between the two domains, where it could threaten the security of Thuringia. Henry VI's main aim at Erfurt was to stop this situation spiralling out of control. Unfortunately, something would break at the meeting, which would lead to this gathering being known as the *Erfurter Latrinensturz* – the Erfurt Latrine Disaster.

The diet was held in the monastic church of St Peter in the citadel of Erfurt. While the church was large enough to host an event where the king, a dozen princes and all their attendants could meet together, the wooden floors could not take the strain of so many gathered at once. If there were alarming creaking noises from the floor, they were ignored by those present. As Henry VI called the meeting to order, the beams supporting the floor failed and sent the assembled nobles crashing down into the floor below. This alone would have been a terrible accident – perhaps not a disaster – but the collapse continued.

Directly below where the diet was being held was the communal toilet used by the monks, in which they defecated into a pit directly beneath. When the waste had filled the pit it would then have been carted away, but it seems that no one had emptied the toilet pit for some time. When the floor above came crashing down, the floor of the toilets gave way too, and the nobles were pitched down again – straight into the latrine pit.

FAILURE TO FLOAT

In 1189, the Holy Roman Emperor Frederick Barbarossa set out on the Third Crusade. While beside the Saleph River in Turkey, he fell into the water and drowned. Whether he tried to swim across in his armour, slipped while bathing, or was thrown by his horse is not clear. However it happened, the emperor drowned in much sweeter water than the nobles at Erfurt.

Henry VI and the Archbishop of Mainz had been standing beside a window when the floor gave way, and they were left clinging on for dear life until they could be rescued by a ladder. Sixty others present were less lucky. Some were mercifully killed by falling debris and died quickly, but others were pitched down into the excrement held in the latrine pit. There they drowned in the fetid pool of waste or were overcome by the built-up gases that settled over the muck. Among the dead were many important counts of the empire and their loyal retainers, but Louis III was pulled alive from the wreckage in the latrine. Both the main disputants had survived, and, in the aftermath of the disaster, the border troubles were settled without further deaths.

THE CRUSADERS FAIL TO REACH JERUSALEM

· ·

The Crusades of the eleventh to thirteenth centuries saw Christian Europeans sailing towards the Holy Land to conquer territories rooted in biblical history. Some simplistic histories of the Crusades paint a picture of united Christianity versus coherent Muslim forces. In fact, the Crusader armies were patchworks of nobles great and small, making and breaking alliances, preachers with different visions of divine glory and common men and women seeking worldly wealth and salvation for their souls. That any Crusader coalitions ever made it to Jerusalem is a miracle.

In 1099, despite great internal tensions, the First Crusade saw the European armies break into the holy city and claim it for Christendom. Instead of falling into pious devotion, the soldiers went on a bloody rampage through the streets, and any Muslims found seeking refuge within mosques were slaughtered where they hid. Chronicles of the time record knights wading through blood up to their ankles, and the dead were so numerous that their bodies were piled higher than buildings when they were burned. The Crusades were always going to be a bloody affair. A kingdom of Jerusalem was declared, and Baldwin of Boulogne was placed on the throne.

Of course, the Islamic peoples, who had governed the area for centuries, were unwilling to allow an interloping state to be formed in their midst. There were various wars fought to capture and recapture the cities of the region, with other crusades called to reinforce the European holdings in the Holy Land. In 1187, Saladin, the Sultan of Egypt and Syria, had managed to drive the Europeans out of Jerusalem, and so it was that the Third Crusade was called in 1189 to retake it. Despite the many deaths incurred and vast sums of money spent on the expedition, Jerusalem remained in Saladin's hands after years of war. The Crusaders did manage to prop up the remaining Christian states in the area and sign a treaty for a three-year peace.

The Third Crusade had laid open the divisions among Christian forces. Frederick Barbarossa, ruler of the Holy Roman Empire, had nearly gone to war with Constantinople when they did not help him cross the Bosphorus on his trek towards Palestine. Though a Christian emperor sat in

Constantinople, many in Europe deemed him the wrong sort, as he followed the Eastern Orthodox faith. There were other tensions between Constantinople and the Crusaders. Crusader armies marching through imperial lands often raided them to feed and enrich themselves.

Constantinople was one of the greatest cities of the age. Founded by the Roman emperor Constantine the Great, it was the heir to Rome's glory. Indeed, the people living there still referred to themselves as Romans and would have been baffled by the idea that the Roman Empire had ever fallen. Thick walls protected it from attack, golden domes towered over the streets and palaces of unrivalled splendour housed the court of the emperor. Guarding the waterways between the Black Sea and the Mediterranean, as well as offering a land bridge between Europe and Asia, had allowed the city to grow rich on trade. Other merchant states, such as the Republic of Venice, resented the way in which Constantinople monopolized the trade routes that it sought.

A Fourth Crusade was launched in 1202 to attack Alexandria in Egypt and weaken the sultan. This target was chosen in order to preserve the treaty signed with regard to Jerusalem, and there were high hopes that the great city of Alexandria would be taken. A powerful city would indeed fall – just not the one that the Crusaders had planned.

To avoid a long march towards the Holy Land, it was agreed that the Crusaders would gather at Venice, where the Venetian fleet would ferry them directly towards their target. Tying up so many ships to transport the expected four thousand five hundred knights, their horses and twenty thousand men at arms would be a costly endeavour, so the Venetians demanded an amount of gold equal to twice the yearly income of the King of England. The terms were agreed upon, so the crusade could proceed.

Unfortunately, fewer soldiers than expected turned up, because many chose to travel from ports other than Venice and the money demanded by the Venetians could not be paid in full. The Crusaders had to change their plans. The Doge of Venice came up with an ingenious way of recouping the losses his city had suffered; first, they would attack the Christian city of Zara on the other side of the Adriatic Sea, to bring it back under Venice's control.

Zara was put under siege, and heavy weapons broke its walls. Inside, the Crusaders battled each other for their share of the loot. This excursion to Zara had delayed the Crusaders, so they spent the winter in their new city. It was while waiting there that they received another tempting offer. Alexios, son of the deposed Emperor Isaac II of Constantinople, was willing to offer extravagant rewards if the Crusaders would attack Constantinople and crown him on the throne his father had occupied. As well as gold and silver, he offered to place the Eastern Orthodox Church under the Pope's control, giving the Crusaders an excuse for considering the attack a holy one undertaken for the Catholic faith. In 1203, they assaulted the city.

The defenders of Constantinople rode out but were repelled by the Crusaders. They rained scalding oil down on the attackers, burning many Crusaders in their armour. The attackers spread fires in which thousands of homes were burned and tens of thousands of inhabitants were left as beggars on the streets. Alexios III, who had usurped the throne from Isaac II, fled the city, allowing Isaac's son,

Alexios, to take charge of the empire as he had planned.

As Alexios IV, the new emperor was unable to pay the debts he had incurred in bribing the Crusaders to place him on the throne. While Constantinople was fabulously rich, the former emperor had managed to escape with most of the treasury. There was also no way that the Orthodox citizens would destroy the icons they used in their worship, as the Catholic Crusaders demanded. The people of Constantinople rioted, the nobility also rose up, and Alexios IV was deposed. Their choice for a new emperor was, confusingly enough, Alexios V.

The new emperor refused to honour any contract that his predecessor might have signed. The Crusaders were left without money and without any of their aims fulfilled. They stormed the city again in 1204 – this time to take the loot for themselves. The Crusaders felt that this was God's will. One said that 'Those who have denied us small things have relinquished everything to us by divine judgement.'

Nothing was spared. Crusaders entered churches and stripped away the gold, silver and jewels that had been left by centuries of worshippers. Many found there was simply too much to carry away and fetched donkeys to load up with booty. Monks accompanying the Crusaders could not resist filling their robes with the treasures they found. Among the most sought-after goods were holy relics. Fingers of St

Thomas that had probed Christ's wound, belts worn by the Virgin and thorns from the Crown of Thorns were shipped back to Europe, alongside secular artistic treasures.

THE BLIND DOGE

By the time the Fourth Crusade set out, Enrico Dandolo, the Doge of Venice, was nearly ninety, and blind. Rumour had it that he was blinded by the Byzantine emperor in Constantinople while visiting the city and this is why Dandolo wished to attack it. Blinding opponents was a Byzantine tactic that they believed to be more merciful than murder. In fact, Dandolo told a contemporaneous chronicler that he had been blinded by a blow to the head in a separate incident long after his trip to Constantinople.

The territory of the Byzantine (Eastern Roman) Empire was also carved up by the Crusaders, and myriad smaller states were shared between the European leaders. The twists and turns of fortune for these lands were byzantine in the extreme, but none ever recaptured the lost glories of the Eastern Roman Empire. The wars and civil wars of the following decades and centuries reduced Constantinople to a shadow of its former self. The Crusaders never did retake Jerusalem, and they had extinguished one of the most flourishing Christian cities in the world.

INALCHUQ FAILS TO SHOW HOSPITALITY

The Khwarazmian Empire is not perhaps the most famous empire in history, but in the early thirteenth century it was one of the most powerful in Central Asia. The rulers of Khwarazm took advantage of the weak seljuk Empire to form their own state and declared themselves to be shahs of equal rank to other kings in the region.

In 1200, Muhammad II came to the Khwarazmian throne and continued to expand his domains. Soon, his armies were taking cities in Afghanistan from neighbouring empires, adding military glory to his sense of pre-eminence. The wealthy trading city of Samarkand, in modern Uzbekistan, also fell to Muhammad II, bringing riches pouring into his treasury. By 1217, Muhammad II was able to threaten the great city of Baghdad itself when the caliph there refused to recognize his authority. So mighty did Muhammad II feel himself to be that he even thought of invading China. Events would overtake the Khwarazmian shah, however, and all due to the failure of one official to greet guests in a proper manner.

The Khwarazmian Empire had the bad luck to reach its zenith at the same time as another power was rising in the east. Genghis Khan had survived a tumultuous childhood among the tribes of the Mongolian steppes. As a young man, he was captured by enemies and came close to death many times, but rose to unite his people. Through the reorganization of the clan system, Genghis found himself in control of hundreds of thousands of loyal warriors. He forged a Mongol Empire that conquered China and began to expand into Central Asia. It was word of these new rulers of China that helped restrain Muhammad II from casting his martial eye in that direction.

The Mongols were not just warrior folk. There were traders and diplomats among their number who travelled to other lands, and in 1218 they crossed into the Khwarazmian Empire. Nomadic people heavily rely on trade for goods they cannot produce themselves, so the lucrative opportunity to trade with such a powerful new empire should have tempted Muhammad II, but he seems to have rebuffed all attempts. His officials were no keener to welcome Mongols.

When a trade caravan of nearly five hundred men with

heavily laden camels arrived in the border town of Otrar, they were also transporting an ambassador sent by Genghis Khan to Muhammad II. They were met by the governor of the town, a relative of the shah called Inalchuq. Instead of aiding the ambassador in his passage towards the capital, Inalchuq had the entire caravan seized and all the men placed under arrest. Inalchuq informed the shah that every member of the caravan was a spy and traitor, so they should be executed, and their goods should be sold. Inalchuq may have thought this would profit him, and it did in the very short term, as the goods raised a fair sum of gold. The Mongol ambassador was publicly executed, in violation of all laws of diplomacy and hospitality, alongside the traders. Only one camel driver managed to escape the slaughter, and it was he who carried word of the butchery back to Genghis.

As history would soon teach the world, it was never a good idea to antagonize the great khan, but in this case he showed some forbearance. He sent another pair of ambassadors to Muhammad II to ask for redress. Muhammad II compounded the error of Inalchuq by beheading one of the ambassadors and cutting the beard from the other, to dishonour him. This was too much. Genghis ordered the wholesale invasion of the Khwarazmian Empire.

Over a hundred thousand Mongols swarmed into Khwarazmian territory. Muhammad II should have realized that his empire was less secure than his successes in battle might have suggested. There were deep divisions in his court, and much power had been placed in the hands of individual generals and governors, while orders from the shah were often disregarded. Many traders who had prosperous relationships with Chinese merchants might have hoped that the Mongols would bring stable peace to the region, so they might have sided with the invaders to escape the shah's ineffective rule.

The Mongols disabused many who hoped for a peaceful takeover. Towns were besieged, and defenders were brutally killed when they fell into Mongol hands. Where the local population had welcomed the invading forces, the people of a town were allowed to exit it, but not to take with them any of their property. Many were also raped and enslaved. Anyone who defied the Mongols in the least way was doomed to death.

At Otrar, where the first ambassador had been killed, the Mongols surrounded the town and waited for it to surrender. Inalchuq, who must have known that his life was forfeit, ordered his men to keep resisting to the last. Not everyone was keen to die for the governor who had brought this disaster on their heads, so one of the gates was opened, and a force of soldiers fled to defect. They were killed out of hand, and the Mongols pushed into the town. Inalchuq and some picked men retreated into the citadel and put up a vigorous defence for another month. Eventually, the Mongols broke in, and Inalchuq retreated ever higher, until he was cornered with nothing to hurl at his enemies but bricks pulled from the walls of the room he was in. The Mongols had been ordered to take Inalchuq alive, and they did, but not out of mercy.

RESPECT FOR ROYALTY

The Mongols believed that royal blood should not be spilled on the ground. When Genghis Khan's grandson Hulego captured Baghdad in 1258, he took the caliph Al-Musta'Sim bi-Ilah alive. To execute the caliph, he was wrapped up in a carpet and trampled by the army and their horses; no noble blood touched the earth.

Inalchuq was dragged before Genghis Khan so that the Mongol could enjoy the death of the man who had given him a reason to go to war. According to some versions, Inalchuq was killed by having molten silver forced down his throat and perhaps into his eyes and ears. Tales of how Inalchuq died may be legendary, but the truth was probably just as spectacularly painful.

Shah Muhammad II saw which way the wind was blowing. He could not muster the armies needed to fight off the invasion and fled with his son, away from the horde descending on him. Muhammad II's flight was disorderly, and he often changed his mind about which fort might offer the best hopes of safety. Eventually, he reached an island where an illness of the lungs carried him off, probably more mercifully than the Mongols would have.

With the Khwarazmian Empire subjugated, the heartlands of the Islamic world were left open for invasion. Many neighbours of Muhammad II would come to rue his failure to find a peaceful resolution to trade negotiations.

A Divine Wind Sinks the Mongol Fleet – Twice

The best-laid plans of even the mightiest of conquerors often go awry for the most banal reasons. Weather can ruin everything from a picnic to an invasion. To have one war fail because of a wind is misfortune, but to have two end in disaster because of a breeze begins to look like carelessness.

By the middle of the thirteenth century, the Mongol Empire had fractured into four distinct khanates. Kublai Khan, the grandson of the great Genghis Khan, had established himself as the ruler of China and declared himself to be the founder of the Yuan dynasty. Through clever diplomacy, wise reforms, and the judicious use of overwhelming military might, he brought more and more territory under his control. After forcing all of Korea to bow to him as a vassal state, the khan began to cast his eye across the sea to Japan and dreamed of also bringing them to heel.

In 1274, hundreds of ships were built in Korea to ferry thousands of Mongol warriors over to Japan. The shogun had prepared for an invasion, but, even so, the numbers of defenders he could muster were insufficient to be certain of victory. We have no precise numbers for the invasion force because histories written by each side saw fit, for reasons that will become clear, to vastly overestimate their opponents.

Based on the first encounter, the Mongols must have expected victory to be swift and easy. After landing, they were met by a couple of dozen samurai, who were soon scattered and killed by the thousands of invaders who waded ashore. The Mongols also had advanced and powerful bows that could slaughter at a greater distance than those of the Japanese. As a final and terrible surprise, the invaders brought explosive charges of gunpowder, which they launched from catapults – the first time such weapons had been seen in Japan. All that would be required of the Mongol forces, it seemed, was to move from island to island and subdue the entire archipelago.

But this never happened. Instead of remaining on land, the Mongol forces had retreated into their ships for the night. This proved to be a terrible blunder. A sudden wind sprang up that drove the hundreds of Mongol ships out to sea and wrecked many of them. The Mongol accounts speak briefly of a storm that ran the ships into rocks and cracked open their hulls. Nearly half of the force never managed to return to Korea.

By 1281, Kublai Khan was in a better position to launch a second and larger invasion of Japan, which he was certain would give him mastery of the country. Having conquered a rival in China, he now had access to a formidable navy and could draw on even more soldiers. Some histories place the Mongol force at four thousand four hundred ships and nearly a hundred and fifty thousand men. They immediately took two small islands to act as staging points for the further invasion of the Japanese home islands.

The Japanese had prepared for a possible attack in the intervening years, however, and at Hakata Bay, where the first invasion landed, a stone wall had been constructed to give shelter to defenders. From behind this edifice, the Japanese launched a withering rain of arrows, which pushed the attackers back to their boats. The Japanese also launched daring raids on the Mongol fleet and managed to make some small victories, but the Mongols were contemptuous of the Japanese ships, which they considered to be nothing but tiny boats. Still, the Mongols lashed their ships together with ropes to provide stable platforms on which to fight back.

Things seemed desperate for the Japanese shogun, despite these early successes. He travelled in person to the temple of Hachiman, a divine entity of warfare, to plead for help. According to Japanese sources, the god answered these prayers.

During the night, a powerful typhoon arose, which churned the waves and sent irresistible gusts of wind down on the Mongol fleet. With so many of the large ships tied together, it was impossible for the sailors to control where they went. Ships collided against each other and shattered the wooden beams. It seemed as if the ships were exploding. Those that did manage to avoid striking other ships were driven onto sharp rocks in the sea and also broken up. Thousands of men were left drifting in rough waters as they clutched to any floating object in the hope of being rescued or swimming ashore. Few were recovered from the water, and most of those who swam to the land were met by Japanese defenders who killed them on sight. Perhaps two thirds of the Mongol forces lost their lives in this way.

JAPANESE DIPLOMACY

During the period between the Mongol invasions, the Chinese sent two groups of emissaries to bring the Japanese to heel. The first group of five were beheaded when they refused to leave Japan without a satisfactory answer. The second five diplomats met the same fate.

The Japanese praised the winds that had twice scattered their enemy as *kamikaze* – divine wind – sent by Hachiman to defend the homeland. The invasions left a strong impression on the Japanese, who fully expected that another might come at any time, and so for decades they kept their defences ready. They never forgot the fate that awaited those who dared to transgress their borders and felt they were assured of divine assistance in times of need. When the Japanese were menaced by American ships during the Second World

War, they again turned to the kamikaze for defence – though in this case they created their own divine wind by sending pilots in explosive planes on suicide missions to collide with enemy vessels.

The Mongols were left significantly weaker at sea than they had been before the invasions. It became obvious that an amphibious assault on Japan would be far more difficult than initially thought. The Mongol emperors continued to try to demand tribute from Japan, but never brought the islands under their control.

MANSA MUSA CRASHES EGYPT'S ECONOMY

There have always been rumours of extraordinarily wealthy empires just beyond the fringes of the known world. It was easy to imagine realms, just beyond the sea, where the streets were paved with gold and potentates lived in palaces glistening with diamonds and rubies. Usually these legends proved to be nothing but the fevered imaginings of fabulists who composed over-the-top travelogues of places they had never been. Sometimes, however, the hearsay turned out to be rather less than the truth.

The empire of Mali in Western Africa, which existed from the thirteenth to the seventeenth centuries, was perfectly positioned to become one of the richest kingdoms in history. The trade routes that connected southern Africa with the north and Europe passed through its borders. With supreme efficiency, every gram of salt, gold and spice was weighed and taxed, with the proceeds going to the king. Besides the profits of trade, Mali also had access to vast gold deposits within its borders. The rulers of Mali did much to hide the location of its gold mines, to discourage any avaricious neighbours from attempting to capture them for themselves, but they could not hide the glittering results. Traders throughout the region knew that a river of gold flowed from Mali. Modern estimates suggest that perhaps half of the gold in the Old World at this time was derived from Mali.

The kings of Mali, known by the title *mansa*, were undoubtedly among the wealthiest individuals who ever lived. In 1324, this ruler was Mansa Musa, who was a devout Muslim. The Mali Empire was one where Islam coexisted with traditional African religions, and Mansa Musa had attempted to spread the influence of Islam. This was not always successful. When he attempted to convert the workers who mined his gold, they refused to extract any more, which led to a sharp decrease in production. Allowing them to return to their old religion brought them back to the mines, and the experiment of conversion was never tried again, lest it reduce the royal income.

It was in 1324 that Mansa Musa decided to make the pilgrimage to Mecca, the *hajj*, which all Muslims are supposed to undertake once in their lives, if they are able. Of course, when the richest man on the planet decides to go on a long expedition, he does not travel alone. According to contemporary accounts, when Musa left Mali he led a caravan of splendour, numbering sixty thousand individuals. Many were decked out in outfits that were layered with gold thread, and his heralds carried staffs made of solid gold. To ensure that there was plenty of money to spend, the king loaded up a hundred camels with thousands of kilos of pure gold.

The pilgrimage convoy crossed North Africa and spread the fame of Mali's wealth far and wide. Traders from across the Muslim and European worlds would have seen the spectacle of innumerable servants bearing an unimaginable fortune in gold and carried word of Musa's journey back to their homes. European maps from the fourteenth century are sometimes illustrated with Mansa Musa as a king holding up the golden treasures of his kingdom.

In Egypt, Mansa Musa's caravan paused in Cairo on its way to Mecca. There, Musa made a favourable impression on the sultan by immediately giving him fifty thousand golden dinars as a gift, but it was not only the high and mighty who were met with golden welcomes. Charity is highly regarded by Muslims, and Musa was going out of his way to prove his Islamic credentials. In Cairo, even the lowliest beggar who came before Musa could expect a small bag of gold dust to relieve their plight.

Of course, when people see money, they will want some for themselves. The merchants of Cairo were not fools, so, whenever they dealt with someone from Mali, they would dramatically raise the asking price for whatever they were selling. Most of the time, their exorbitant demands were met with immediate payment in gold.

LOST AT SEA

Mansa Musa described how one of his predecessors built a fleet of ships and sailed westwards into the Atlantic Ocean in search of new lands, but failed to return. Did his navy reach the New World, or was it wrecked and now lies under the ocean? The latter seems more likely. After this experiment in ocean-crossing, the empire of Mali focused on its dominance in trade.

Gold had long been the ultimate mark of wealth in much of the world: it is beautiful, never tarnishes and is rare. Europe, in particular, had very few sources of native gold, so there was always a chronic shortage, and silver was the more common form of bullion and coin. The relative values of silver and gold, therefore, had a major impact on the economic systems of most nations. Suddenly, thanks to the generosity of Musa and his entourage, there was a flood of gold into the Egyptian market, and from there into much of the Islamic world and Europe. The value of gold was heavily depressed. Gold lost some of the lustre it once had now that so many had managed to get their hands on some.

Musa continued on his pilgrimage and duly wowed everyone who met him with his wealth and power. However, even the largest fortune can be exhausted if you continue to give it away. On the journey back to Mali, the bags of gold on his camels began to empty. Soon the pilgrims found that they had no money to sustain them on their return, and to finance the rest of the trip, many had to borrow back some of the gold they had paid out. Others were forced to sell the goods they had spent lavishly on in Egypt for a fraction of their value. Once back in Mali, all these losses were made good by the wealth of the kingdom.

In Egypt, problems were less easy to fix. It is hard to get detailed figures on exactly how deeply Musa's spending spree suppressed the price of gold, but by some accounts, it took the economy there decades to recover from its encounter with the wealth of Mali.

China Turns its Back on Exploration, and Declines

. . . .

In 1405, a grand banquet was held by the Yongle Emperor of the Ming dynasty to honour the commanders and crew of the most remarkable naval venture in Chinese history, known as the treasure fleets. The emperor had financed the construction of huge ships, gathered tens of thousands of sailors, and ordered them to travel into the West. There they were to deliver imperial messages and gifts for the rulers of the nations they encountered. On their return, the treasure fleet was to bring back tributes to the emperor from the new peoples they encountered.

Some of the treasure ships were among the largest wooden vessels ever to set sail. The biggest were said to be 140 m (459 ft) long and 50 m (164 ft) wide, and could carry immense loads of trade goods in their hold. These behemoths of the waves were supported by dozens of smaller ships. To witness a treasure fleet descending on a port unused to such sights must have been like seeing aliens arriving from a distant world.

Over seven voyages, the treasure fleets under the command of admiral Zheng He explored the Indian Ocean and beyond. We have reports of their visits to the Indian coast, Sri Lanka, Sumatra, Yemen, the Persian Gulf, the ports of Somalia and Jedda. Along the way, the fleet had time to destroy the swarms of pirates that threatened Chinese trade, and to depose the King of Ceylon, who proved to be unwelcoming to Chinese influence.

Each time the fleet returned to China, it brought emissaries from each of the destinations it had visited that carried with them messages from their rulers and gifts of tribute to the emperor. So massive was the diplomatic importance of these voyages, that an institute was created in China to foster the study of foreign languages to smooth communication at the meetings. The envoys would be sent home with more gifts to strengthen the ties that had been forged.

We know of the extraordinary wealth in rare and exotic items that flowed into China from the voyages of the fleet. Spices, gold and fabulous textiles were among the least of the gifts that the Yongle Emperor found falling into his hands – there are records of giraffes, cheetahs, lions, ostriches and rhinos being carried back to China.

The military might of the treasure fleets, and their

intervention in local politics when they found conditions were not favourable to China, reveals that they were not sent out purely as a show of force. They were the force itself that China wished to project to the wider world. The Ming dynasty at this point had only recently been established, after driving out the Mongol rulers who had failed to quell rebellions against their rule. By looking outwards, they hoped to cement their place as one of the most powerful kingdoms in their region, and bring ever greater wealth and influence to the imperial throne.

The Yongle Emperor could not place all his attention on the wider world, however, as there were threats closer to home. The Mongols still controlled large areas to the north of the Ming domains, and relations with their neighbours were fraught. The Chinese thought that the Mongols should submit to them and offer tribute, while the Mongols had a habit of executing the diplomats sent to them by the Ming court. Resources were required to fight the wars that broke out between the two at regular intervals, and the treasure fleets, while spectacular, were also spectacularly expensive. In 1421, after the sixth voyage, the sailing of the fleets was suspended. Zheng He was appointed to garrison duty, and the fleets set out to secure the sea borders of China.

The seventh and final fleet was sent out by the Xuande Emperor, when he ascended the throne, as a way of reminding those rulers who had offered submission to the former emperor that China was still a great power under its new ruler. Following the fleet's return, internal opposition to what many considered a wasteful endeavour grew, and there was not to be another expedition. China turned inwards to focus on domestic problems and defend its borders. Soon, the Ming reconstruction of the Great Wall would call on incredible amounts of material and manpower to keep the Mongol invaders from the homeland, and there was little left for exploration.

The treasure fleets did not break new ground in terms of Chinese exploration of the ocean, as there was already a well-developed network of sea trade that allowed them to follow maps to their destinations. Their success came in projecting Chinese power over a wider area than ever before, and knitting far, disparate lands into a more connected world.

There have been some fringe scholars who have posited that the treasure fleets may have visited Australia and even North America. This seems unlikely as their routes are well documented, and no firm evidence has ever been presented to support these claims. If the treasure fleets had not been stopped, there can be little doubt that they would have visited further and more distant locations. Who can say what discoveries might have been made? Knowledge of Chinese technological advances and culture might have played a greater role in world history.

THE EUNUCH ADMIRAL

Zheng He came from a Muslim family and, after his capture by Ming forces as a young boy, he was castrated to enter the service of the Yongle Emperor. Eunuchs were entrusted with many positions of power at the Ming court, and Zheng He stood out for his skill as a soldier, administrator and diplomat. He was also said to stand out physically, because of his reputed height of seven feet (2.1 m).

Urban the Hungarian is not Hired by Constantinople

By the 1450s, the Byzantine Empire was not the power it had once been. Repeated civil wars left it underpowered and underpopulated. Once legendary, its wealth was spent, and little was left to maintain even the facade of its former greatness. The shattered remnants of its domains had split from the capital at Constantinople and been conquered piecemeal, principally by the rising Ottoman Empire. Only the mighty walls of the city held back the waves of destruction that were preparing to wash over what had become the last outpost of the mighty Roman Empire.

In 1453, the Ottomans, under the conquering warrior Sultan Mehmed II, were ready to invade the tiny holdings of the Byzantines and even take Constantinople itself. It was then that a travelling bronze-worker named Urban presented himself to the court of the Byzantine emperor, Constantine XI Palaiologos. Most European monarchs supported artists who worked with bronze to cast medallions and statues, but Urban was offering a quite different product. He knew the skill of creating large bombards from bronze that could blast heavy stones over long distances. These cannons had been largely abandoned in other places because smaller cannons made of iron were easier to build and transport, though they lacked the firepower of the bombard.

Constantine XI was duly impressed with Urban's weapons of war, but there was hardly any money left in his treasury to support Urban's plans. The Byzantines lacked even the raw materials to build the bombards that Urban promised to make for them. They might have melted down bronze statues to turn into cannons, but there was not enough wood to power the foundries. Chronicles of the time say that the emperor ordered that a small stipend be paid to Urban to keep him in the city – but even this was withheld. This failure to keep Urban on side shaped the whole, and short, future of the Byzantine Empire.

Urban was placed into destitution by attaching himself to the court without pay. When he could no longer stand his poverty, Urban slipped out of Constantinople and presented himself to Mehmed II, who immediately saw the benefits of working with him. The Ottoman ruler questioned Urban and asked whether he could create a cannon large enough to blast through the strong walls of the city. Urban had no shortage of belief in his creations. If Mehmed provided him with the materials, he said, then he could build a bombard that would reduce the walls of Babylon itself to dust. What was more, Urban had taken the time to study the walls of the city closely during his unemployment, and knew just where to target his stones. Mehmed funded the making of a colossal cannon.

Within three months, the Ottomans found themselves in possession of one of the largest weapons ever built. Mehmed had the artillery set up near his palace in Adrianople and charged with gunpowder. Before test-firing the cannon, the emperor warned the inhabitants of the city what was about to happen, lest the shock cause pregnant women to miscarry.

When fired, the cannon launched a heavy stone over 1.5 km (just under a mile), and the blast could be heard at a distance of 16 km (10 miles). The Ottomans prepared to besiege Constantinople.

It took two months, thirty wagons and sixty muscular oxen to drag the bombard the short distance to the city, where it would be fired at the gates. On first hearing the thunderous noise of the cannon blasting, the inhabitants of the city cried out to God for mercy. The slow rate of fire gave the defenders time to repair much of the damage, but the cannon continued pounding the wall for weeks. Urban used the cannon to target the towers surrounding the gates and, with a final shot, sent them all tumbling to the ground.

The Ottomans mobilized all their forces for a final assault on the city. Some targeted the breaches in the walls, while others scaled ladders to open multiple fronts. The defenders fought bravely, but were no match for the overwhelming numbers of the Ottomans. Emperor Constantine XI is said to have cast off his imperial regalia to join the fighting in front of the walls of his city. No record was made of his final moments, but he is said to have scorned the idea of surviving as an emperor without an empire.

LENDING EXPERTISE IS A MISTAKE

States were well aware that it was dangerous to allow experts in weapon-making to be captured by their enemies. When Mehmed II asked Venice to send him bronze-workers to create art, the city refused to comply, lest they be used to further bolster Mehmed's arsenal.

Christian chroniclers recounted tales of the brutal sacking that followed the fall of Constantinople. Those sheltering in churches found no hope of salvation as soldiers broke in with their swords drawn. Thousands were slaughtered, children were captured and taken as slaves and all of the remaining wealth that could be found anywhere in the ancient city was carried away as plunder.

The fall of Constantinople shocked Europe. It had been a bastion against the Islamic forces that terrified Christian leaders across the continent. Pope Pius II thought that it was necessary to call for another crusade to stop the Ottomans from making any further inroads into Europe, but this proposed venture never happened.

For want of a small salary that might have been paid out of the gold plate which the emperor in Constantinople no doubt ate from every day, the Byzantine Empire sped the destruction of its walls and last defences. Without Urban passing to the Ottomans, would Constantinople have fallen? Probably, but it remains a tantalizing possibility that the Byzantines might have withstood long enough for other opportunities to arise.

COLUMBUS MISCALCULATES THE WORLD

· ·

Christopher Columbus's discovery in 1492 of a route from Europe westward over the Atlantic to fabulous new lands is one of the most successful naval voyages ever undertaken. Unfortunately, from his own point of view, it was an utter failure, even though he could never admit to that.

Columbus's aim in mounting the expedition was to find a relatively simpler route to the Indies – the fantastically wealthy regions of China and India. Existing passages required thousands of kilometres of land crossing, so a quicker route could yield untold riches.

A well-known anecdote about Columbus is that he faced huge disapproval as he set out on his voyage because he alone in Europe knew that the world was round. Every other navigator thought the Earth was flat, so to sail west would risk falling off the edge of the world. But there were other reasons to oppose Columbus's planned voyage.

Indeed, by the fifteenth century, most educated people in Europe had accepted that the world was spherical. Ancient Greek scholars had used the position of the sun to calculate the size of Earth's sphere. Eratosthenes managed, in the third century BC, to come up with a reasonably accurate measurement by placing sticks in the ground and noting how long their shadows were at different places on the same day.

The real reason many educated people believed Columbus was setting an impossible task in sailing west to reach the Far East was that they understood just how far away it is. Columbus alone miscalculated how long such a journey would take. In fact, Columbus didn't just make a single error in his calculations – he made several catastrophic blunders.

Columbus based his estimate of the size of the globe on the work of Alfraganus, an Arabic scholar from the ninth century. Alfraganus's work was far ahead of its time, but Columbus mistranslated his measurements. Instead of using the Arabic mile, which equalled over 7,000 feet, Columbus used the Roman mile, which was only 4,856 feet. This effectively shrank the globe by around a quarter. Additionally, Columbus believed Asia to be far larger and closer to Europe than it is. It may be that he had heard rumours that Northern European sailors had occasionally spotted land when fishing in the North Atlantic.

For these reasons, Columbus became unshakeably convinced that sailing across the Atlantic to Asia was a trivial affair and that all he needed to attempt it was to convince someone to fund a fleet. His first port of call was Portugal. The Portuguese at this time were among the most powerful naval powers in Europe. They had already sent expeditions southward along the coast of Africa and were busy mapping routes to determine whether there was a sea passage around its southern tip that would lead to the Indian Ocean. They had also discovered trade winds from Africa that reached far out into the Atlantic, which a bold mariner would be able to exploit.

The Portuguese were keen to access the spice islands of Asia, but their knowledge of overland routes had given them a good idea of Asia's size. They also knew Columbus to be wrong about its location relative to Europe. King John II of Portugal's advisors recognized that Columbus' estimate of the distance between Europe and Asia was only a quarter of the real figure. To add to Columbus' woes was the news that Bartolomeu Dias had rounded the Cape of Good Hope, giving his native Portugal a way to sail into the Indian Ocean. Columbus' plan was rejected.

Columbus next appealed to the court of Ferdinand and Isabella in Spain. Again, their most knowledgeable advisors declared Columbus' plan mistaken in many key points. To stop him from taking his plan elsewhere, he was kept around the court on a pension, but it appeared that his journey would never happen. Only after several years did the Spanish monarchs decide that the potential for great returns outweighed the relatively small cost of the voyage, reasoning that should Columbus disappear at sea, they would not suffer a great loss.

In 1492, Columbus set out from Spain with three ships: the *Santa Maria*, the *Pinta* and the *Santa Clara*, known to its sailors as the *Nina*. They sailed with nothing but ocean waves surrounding them for over a month, so Columbus was forced to put down a potential mutiny when his crews became concerned that they might never again see land. However, soon after this, they spotted birds and objects floating in the water and correctly surmised that their journey was nearing its end. Columbus had promised a huge reward to anyone who sighted land first. Rodrigo de Triana was the first to cry out but never received any money because Columbus claimed to have already seen land the previous night and had just not told anybody.

Columbus' voyage was simultaneously a success and a failure. To the end of his life, Columbus was convinced that the land he discovered was part of Asia, despite there being no sign of the expected peoples of India, China or Japan. Columbus reported to Ferdinand and Isabella that the islands he found were just off the coast of China, and he called the people he 'discovered' Indians. For them, the arrival of Europeans in the New World was to prove a terrible disaster.

SUSPICIONS AND BROKEN SHIPS

When the rudder of the *Pinta* was damaged after just three days at sea, the crew suspected it had been sabotaged by the ship's owners, who might have heard about Columbus's miscalculations and feared it would never return from the journey.

MUSLIM KINGDOMS
LOSE IBERIA

· ·

In AD 711, a small army led by Tariq ibn Ziyad crossed from North Africa to modern day Spain and defeated the king of the Visigoths, who ruled much of Iberia. This was to be the beginning of seven centuries of Muslim rule over much of the peninsula. The region was declared to be a province of the greater Umayyad Caliphate, which stretched from the borders of India to the Atlantic Ocean.

The Spanish portion of this empire became known as Al-Andalus, and it would form one of the most unique cultural melting pots in the medieval world. Alongside the Muslim rulers, there were large Jewish communities and a greater number of Christians. Influences flowed into the region from across the caliphate, creating a novel breeding ground for art, literature, science and learning.

Much of Europe at this point had little access to the works of Greek classical scholarship, while, in the Arabic world, the knowledge of the Greeks had been preserved, commented on and expanded. The latest scientific equipment, such as astrolabes and medical tools, was crafted in Al-Andalus. The study of mathematics was improved, and the Arabic numerals still used in much of Europe were introduced. Philosophical texts were copied and translated into many languages, which helped disperse learning both ancient and modern. Universities flourished, and learned figures flocked to Al-Andalus to study works that were available nowhere else. Pope Sylvester II had studied in Al-Andalus in the tenth century and was renowned for his knowledge and wisdom – though some claimed he had also learned the dark arts of magic there.

Historians look back on the centuries of Muslim rule in Al-Andalus as a successful experiment in multiculturalism. They term it the *Convivencia* (literally, 'living together') thanks to the relative peace between its Christians, Jews and Muslims, who coexisted with remarkable tolerance for each other. This may be too rosy a picture, as there were occasional waves of repression against non-Muslim inhabitants of the region that saw waves of emigration by Jews and Christians, but for long periods there was prosperity for the peoples of Al-Andalus.

It was not a time of total peace, either. Various caliphates rose and fell; there were civil wars between competing regions of Al-Andalus, and splits into smaller kingdoms. There were many rulers in Europe who were far from happy to have people they regarded as infidels keep a foothold in Spain. There was also the small Christian kingdom of Asturias in the north of Spain, which would have been very happy to cast out the Moorish invaders.

The end of Al-Andalus came on slowly and was caused by

a series of failures to unite in the face of emboldened Christian forces. In the eleventh century, Pope Urban II, who launched the first crusade to recapture Jerusalem, was also a strong supporter of a crusade in Iberia to drive out the Muslim forces there. As the region split into rival states, some of them fairly small, they became rivals to each other and would fight with each other even as other Christian kingdoms arose in newly liberated lands such as Aragon, Leon and Castile. The petty kingdoms of the Muslims were known to double-cross each other, pay tribute to the Christians and scheme relentlessly to gain any advantage over their neighbours. Yet this was also a high point of culture, with the many rival courts offering patronage to many scholars and artisans.

This period of advance by the Christian kingdoms is known as the *Reconquista* ('reconquest'). The small states of Al-Andalus lacked the strength and unity to offer much resistance. One by one they fell, as their rulers failed to put up adequate defences against the coming Christians.

The final Muslim kingdom in Iberia was the Emirate of Granada. Its survival was helped by Castile becoming focused on internal issues, so that peace was maintained for several decades. The Christian kingdom of Aragon also offered a chance for peace, as Granada was able to play the two potential enemies off against each other. This peace gave rise to the final flourishing of the culture that had developed in

Al-Andalus. Conversely, the external peace left the powerful members of the court at Granada the time and opportunity to launch coups against their leaders and partake in intense political manoeuvring.

THE ALHAMBRA CHANGES HANDS

The Alhambra palace of the Emirs of Granada became a royal palace for Ferdinand and Isabella. It was there that the monarchs met with Christopher Columbus to arrange the details of his planned voyage to Asia.

The fall of Granada came when Isabella of Castile and Ferdinand of Aragon married and united their kingdoms. Now Granada had only one enemy: Spain's new rulers were staunch supporters of the Catholic faith and determined to drive out the last of the Muslims. Other Christian nations in Europe were encouraged by the Pope to lend their assistance. Over a decade of war, the borders of Granada were pushed ever further backwards, until only the city of Granada, hiding behind its own walls, remained.

In 1492, with the Spanish laying siege to the city, a treaty was signed that handed over the last part of Al-Andalus to Isabella and Ferdinand. The once magnificent experiment in toleration was at an end, with the most important Muslim leaders fleeing to North Africa.

Months later, the Spanish monarchs signed the Alhambra Decree, which ordered all Jews to leave their kingdom. Anyone who wished to remain was forced to convert to Catholicism. Muslims were initially dealt with more charitably, but they too were eventually told to convert or leave. Even those who converted were not totally safe, and for centuries were treated with suspicion as potentially still clinging to their old faiths. The Spanish Inquisition was invited to investigate these people with ruthless intensity.

The fall of Al-Andalus was the rise of a very dark time for many in Iberia.

EUROPEAN DISEASES RAVAGE THE NEW WORLD

Following the European discovery of the New World in the 1490s, there was a great rush by many nations to see what economic and political power could be extracted from it. The Columbian Exchange, as the trade in products between the Old and New Worlds is known, saw crops, animals and natural products crossing the Atlantic, as well as the magnificent artistic creations of the native peoples sent home as trinkets.

By the sixteenth century, vast Spanish treasure fleets ferried thousands of tonnes of silver from mines in Bolivia and Mexico. This influx of precious metals helped to prop up the Habsburg monarchy of Spain in the face of massive debts, and it also reorganized the entire economy of the planet. As trade with China developed, Europeans paid for most goods with silver bullion that could largely be traced back to the New World. While Europe benefited, many in the New World suffered from the trade across the Atlantic.

Christopher Columbus treated the native inhabitants of the Caribbean brutally as he searched for a source of gold. He also thought that the Taíno people he found there would make excellent slaves. He tried to export some of them back to Spain, but many died on the crossing. Later, the indigenous peoples would be turned to work on the estates that Europeans established in their new domains. This was necessary for the Europeans, as even in the rush of European adventurers seeking to make their fortune in the New World, the population of native peoples dwarfed the few colonists.

What early European settlers did not recognize was that

they were transporting something more dangerous than guns and troops to the New World – they were bringing diseases that had never been encountered there before. Diseases such as smallpox, typhus and measles had long been endemic in the Old World, and, though deadly, many European populations had developed at least some level of natural immunity to them. They had also created a system of treatment that, though rudimentary by modern standards, did mitigate some of the effects and limit the spread of the diseases. The indigenous peoples of the New World, however, had never experienced anything like these infections.

Atlantic crossings from Europe were undertaken in cramped conditions with limited opportunities for hygiene, so that if even one colonist was infected with a disease, soon the whole ship could be carrying it. When they disembarked in the New World, they spread whatever diseases they had. By some accounts, in the century after European contact with the Americas the native population declined by 90 per cent, and this was mostly due to disease transmission. This represents tens of millions of people who died from illnesses they had never encountered before, and they must have seemed like an act of God, striking them with no obvious cause. The Taíno people that Columbus was so enthusiastic about enslaving were virtually wiped out.

The collapse of populations had dramatic effects on the fate of European colonization. Hernán Cortés had set out to conquer the Aztec Empire in 1519 without official orders, and so a second Spanish force was sent to turn Cortés back. They failed to stop Cortés, but they did introduce smallpox to the mainland. It spread rapidly, weakened the Aztec Empire, and contributed to its defeat by the conquistadors. Many in the Aztec armies died outright, the deaths of commanders left their forces without leadership, and those who recovered from the disease were disfigured and weakened, offering far less resistance to European adventurers.

The monk Toribio de Benavente had travelled to New Spain, as the Aztec Empire became, in 1523, and he witnessed the failure of native societies in the face of epidemics. He recounted how the people there succumbed and died where they lay, in heaps of corpses 'like bedbugs'. In heart-rending scenes, he describes how many young people died of starvation, as there were so few left to tend to them. When whole families perished, the people simply pulled their homes down on top of them to create makeshift tombs. The deaths of those the Europeans put to work were exacerbated by the harsh conditions in many of the mines and plantations they erected.

The epidemics that ravaged the New World were a disaster, not only for the native peoples. The Europeans required a workforce if they were to exploit the new opportunities they found there, and the workers had to be found somewhere. The Spanish and Portuguese had imported Africans to be used as slaves before Columbus discovered the New World, so it was to Africa that they turned to populate their new holdings.

A KING'S RANSOM

South America did have vast resources of gold and silver that could be called upon. When the explorer Francisco Pizarro captured the Inca leader Atahualpa in 1532, he was promised enough gold to fill a large room once over, and enough silver to fill it twice over. Before the full ransom could be paid, Pizarro executed Atahualpa. This has led to the legend of the treasure of Llanganatis, said to be the rest of the promised precious metal that was buried following the slaying of Atahualpa.

Over 12 million Africans would end up being captured, forced onto dangerously cramped vessels in horrific conditions, and sold to Europeans in the New World.

Most of these enslaved people were put to work on sugar plantations and other agricultural estates and, with hardly any legal rights, endured treatment that few can imagine. Given the huge numbers of enslaved Africans who died from mistreatment and disease, the slave trade had to continually bring more people from the Old World to the New. The profits of the labour extracted from slaves were used to purchase more slaves.

Some failures cannot be blamed on anyone. The Europeans who conquered the New World may have intended nothing good for the indigenous peoples, but they did not knowingly spread their diseases. The peoples of the New World just had no effective methods of preventing these epidemics. Sometimes failure is simply inevitable.

THE CATHOLIC CHURCH FAILS TO REFORM

On 31 October 1517, the German theologian Martin Luther is said to have strode up to All Saints' Church in Wittenberg and nailed his Ninety-Five Theses, which criticized many contemporary practices of the Catholic Church, to the door. This act is considered by many to be the beginning of the

Protestant Reformation, which would tear Europe apart in the following centuries.

The Church in Rome under the papacy had been remarkably successful at stamping its authority over the nations of Western Europe up to this point. With a strict hierarchy that ranged from local priests to bishops, cardinals and even the Pope himself, the Church exerted moral and political control in a way that crossed borders. Kings and queens may have sat on the throne, but all of them were thought to have been appointed by God, and the Pope was God's representative on Earth, so he had extraordinary power and influence. The threat of excommunication, banning people from participating in Church rites, had brought more than one monarch on their knees before St Peter's throne.

The Popes could call on the loyalty of millions of Christians because it was held that salvation, and therefore eternal paradise, could only be gained through obedience to Catholic doctrine. Europe in the sixteenth century was a profoundly religious time so religion was the arbiter of truth, not science.

One of the methods a person used to prove their devotion to God was to offer gifts and donations to the Church. Many wills show large amounts of land and money being given to abbeys and religious institutions. These gifts were often left with the instruction that masses be held for the benefit of the dead person's soul. Other people would undertake pilgrimages to holy sites for remission of their sins and would purchase small mementos of their voyages. Besides these occasional donations, the faithful were also expected to regularly offer up a tenth of their income to the Church as a tithe. The Church could draw on these revenues to raise enormous amounts of cash to fund its activities.

It is easy to see how such large financial dealings could lead to greed and corruption. It was not uncommon for priests to hold several positions from which they could make an income, and they would then pay lesser sums to poorly educated replacement priests to perform their duties in their absence. Ecclesiastical abuses such as this led to some complaints, but there was little the average person could do. Clergy were afforded the right to only be tried by Church courts.

Of course, the Church had enormous expenditures that were often greater than its income, so to raise greater sums, the Church offered the sale of indulgences. These were pieces of paper, which could be purchased from travelling salesmen, that offered to reduce the amount of time a person would have to spend in purgatory after death before being allowed into heaven. It was to finance the building of St Peter's Basilica in Rome that one seller of indulgences was active in Germany in the early sixteenth century.

Johann Tetzel arrived near Wittenberg with a stack of indulgences, which he could sell in a carnival of forgiveness. It was said that as soon as a coin fell into his coffer, a soul would fly out of purgatory. This was the nakedly avaricious practice that provoked Luther to write his theses against the whole business of indulgences.

UN-HOLY MONEY

The papacy could use financial means to exert temporal control. When Philip II launched his naval Armada against Protestant England, it was with the promise of 1 million ducats from Pope Sixtus V. The Pope reneged on this promise in the aftermath of the Armada's failure, as the invasion force technically never landed in England.

Luther sparked a revolution in Europe with his challenge to the papacy's ability to raise money. In previous centuries, those who spoke out against the Church would only have been able to influence small numbers of people because it was hard for news to spread. Heretic sects, such as the Lollards, Hussites and Waldensians, attracted some followers but never seriously challenged the power of the Church. The Church acted as if Luther was simply another rogue preacher who could be contained, as so many in the past had been. They had failed to factor in the role of the printing press and the ease with which new ideas could spread.

For a text to be copied in earlier times, it required a great deal of effort for a scribe to make the copy and a lot of money to buy the materials. Only those works deemed worthy of duplication were made in large numbers, and many scribes worked for religious institutions, meaning the Church could easily exert control over printed texts. But with cheap paper and moveable type, hundreds of pamphlets could be produced relatively cheaply in days.

Luther had a good relationship with the printing press attached to the university where he taught, and he understood the power of the written word. Within a few years, his works, ever more stridently attacking all aspects of papal authority, were being read across the continent. Copies were burned in many marketplaces, but there were always more emerging from the presses. It was impossible for the old forms of repression to deal with the new technology.

Many in Europe suddenly became aware that it was possible to question the Church's teachings on all manner of subjects. They might even be able to own a copy of the Bible in their language and make up their own mind about its contents. Protestant sects sprang up all over Europe as the Church failed to offer any reforms to its practices that might lessen its position as the ultimate authority, or threaten its finances. The centuries that followed were stained with the blood of martyrs on both sides of the Reformation.

The Spanish Armada Gets
Blown Off Course

· ·

In 1588, Philip II of Spain was the most powerful monarch in Europe. His domains included Portugal, the Netherlands, Naples, Sicily, huge swathes of the Americas and the Philippines. While he was married to Queen Mary I, he had also been co-monarch of England. When she died in 1558, however, the throne passed to Mary's half-sister Elizabeth, and the stage was set for one of the grandest naval invasions ever planned.

Henry VIII, father of Mary and Elizabeth, had begun the separation of the English and Roman churches when he declared himself to be head of the Church of England. This was so that Henry could grant himself an annulment of his marriage to Catherine of Aragon, mother of Mary, and marry Anne Boleyn, mother of Elizabeth. The separation of the churches allowed aspects of the Protestant Reformation to creep into English religious life. When the crown passed to Mary, she did all she could to return England to its ancient Catholic faith and was aided in this by her pious husband, Philip.

The marriage between England and Spain produced no heirs, so Elizabeth, who was minded to side with reformers, inherited the throne after Mary died. Philip considered Elizabeth I to be a mere bastard of Henry VIII, and therefore illegitimate. Fortunately for Elizabeth, England was a small nation, with little to entice Philip into invading to cast her down.

This changed as English ships started to plunder Spanish fleets in the New World. The Spanish Crown was heavily indebted, requiring frequent infusions of gold and silver from its empire to pay back the European bankers it regularly borrowed from. Any disruption to this flow could not be tolerated. The English also sent aid to the Low Countries, which were in open rebellion against the Spanish Crown. As well as being an important trading partner for England, the Dutch were Protestant allies against the might of Catholic Spain. Spain could not afford to allow the upstart English to interfere in their imperial affairs, so a plan for invasion was drawn up.

The *Grande y Felicísima Armada* (the Great and Fortunate Fleet) that Spain gathered together consisted of a hundred and fifty ships and nearly twenty thousand soldiers – the largest fleet ever seen in Europe. The ships bristled with cannons. While many were merchant ships that had been outfitted for war, there were also large and specially constructed warships that could outgun anything in the English navy. The English had more ships, but they were not of the same class as the Spanish vessels. The aim of sending the Armada was either to invade England or to threaten it to such an extent that Philip could force England to withdraw from European politics. The Pope also lent his support by declaring the invasion of England to be a crusade that would help rid Europe of heretics.

The Armada sailed towards the Netherlands, to pick up thousands more soldiers for the invasion. The English nearly faced disaster when the Spanish fleet trapped them in Portsmouth harbour – had the Spanish struck then, no force could have prevented the invasion – but the Spanish commander had orders not to engage and to carry on for the Netherlands. The English dogged the Armada along the channel but could not get close, lest the Spanish destroy them at close quarters with their superior cannons. The English did manage to capture one lagging Spanish ship and take its sorely needed supplies of money and gunpowder.

When the Armada anchored off Calais, the English menaced them with fireships. These were ships packed with flammable material that were set loose to drift into the tightly packed Armada. They created havoc as the Armada scattered to avoid them, and the next day, in the confusion, the English attacked. Several of the Armada ships were badly damaged and others captured, but it remained a formidable force. The greater risk came from the shallow waters they were sheltering in, which might have left them stranded when the tide went out.

The commanders of the Armada met in council to discuss the disarray they found themselves in. It was decided that the Armada had failed, and the best hope was to sail for Spain and safety. Some captains tossed cannons overboard, lightening their load as they would no longer be needed in an invasion and reducing the risk of being beached. The only question was which route the fleet would take home. The Channel was still swarming with English ships, though the Spanish did not know that their enemies had nearly run out of gunpowder. It was decided to sail north around the top of the British Isles and thence south to Spain.

English ships shadowed the Spanish until they reached Scotland, when they returned to their home ports to announce the ruinous state of their foes. The Spanish were quickly running short of food and water and lacked maps of the areas they were sailing through when the weather turned against them. Fogs rose up and gales surged around the ships. As the fleet sailed around Ireland, at least twenty-five ships were wrecked and their sailors drowned in the churning sea.

News of the Armada's utter failure sent the Spanish court into mourning, while the English lit bonfires to celebrate their great deliverance from peril. English Protestants declared this an act of God and a clear sign that He was on their side.

The Armada became a feature of English propaganda and iconography. Portraits of Elizabeth I were commissioned showing the wreck of the Spanish fleet, and medals struck with the words 'God blew, and they were scattered'.

For the Spanish, the Armada was a costly debacle: Philip II was forced to borrow heavily and at exorbitant rates of interest. Despite this, the Armada of 1588 is only the most famous of a number he planned. Spain sent four more fleets to attack England in the following years – and each failed just as decisively.

CAREFUL WITH YOUR CANDLES

Serving on a naval vessel of this era was always risky. Before the Armada had even reached the Netherlands, thousands of sailors had died from disease. Accidents could be disastrous, and any naked flame on a ship was a hazard. The *San Salvador*'s supply of gunpowder exploded while not engaged in battle, killing fifty of the crew. It was set adrift after the rest of the crew was rescued.

THE SONGHAY EMPIRE FALLS BECAUSE CATTLE CHARGE THE WRONG WAY

· ·

In English idiom, Timbuktu has come to symbolize a place that is far away from anywhere, but it once stood as the most flourishing city in one of the great empires of Africa. The Songhay Empire, centred on the Niger River, ruled much of West Africa and had prospered as the empire of Mali dissolved. Trade flowed along the Niger and thence overland to the north, where it passed into the Mediterranean. The gold mines of the Songhay fed many hungry economies in Europe. Where one nation has wealth, however, many will eye it greedily and want to take it from them.

The Sultan of Morocco, Ahmad al-Mansur, was riding high when he took the throne in 1578. Morocco had just beaten back a Portuguese army and captured many important prisoners who were freed only in return for hefty ransoms. The overflowing treasury chests funded lavish building works and a strong army – until they started to run out. The sultan decided that, if his nation was to continue to thrive, he would have to seize the trade routes that produced the most gold, and turned his eyes south towards the Songhay. However, his threats of war and demands for money were met with scorn. As a sign that his horsemen were ready for any invasion, the Songhay leader Ishaq II mockingly sent the sultan horseshoes.

The Songhay Empire was a highly developed state, but perhaps it should not have been so confident in its military prowess. At this point in history, rebellions in several of its towns and provinces reduced the manpower it could call on to defend itself when the Sultan of Morocco sent an invasion force to push the teetering Songhay into total collapse.

The army sent by the sultan in 1591 was absurdly small for one aiming to overthrow an empire, consisting of somewhere between four thousand and fifteen thousand men. The Songhay could call up many times this number and had the advantage of knowing the land they would fight on. It should have been a relatively simple matter to send the Moroccans back the way they had come, or to leave their bones bleaching in the sun.

Had Ishaq II been less certain of victory, it is possible that the Moroccan soldiers would never have reached his lands. As it was, the journey they undertook was perilous, and more than one army in the region had died from lack of water. Had Ishaq sent troops to guard the wells, or blocked or poisoned them, then the sultan's men would have had no choice but to turn back or die. The Songhay did not even post scouts on the most obvious routes, so the arrival of the Moroccan army came as a surprise. Thus, it was a hastily gathered Songhay force that met the invaders.

The Songhay's army was strong in both cavalry and spearmen and probably many times the size of their enemy when the two sides met at Tondibi, a cattle pasture not far from the capital city of Gao. The Songhay strategy was to round up a thousand of the cattle, force them to stampede at the Moroccans, and scatter them. The infantry would then follow in their wake and slay the Moroccans in their disarray.

This plan was undone by the failure of the Songhay to account for advances in warfare. The vast Moroccan expenditure on their armies had supplied their soldiers with modern firearms and cannons, while the Songhay still relied on weapons that now belonged to an earlier age.

When battle was engaged, the Songhay drove their cattle directly at the Moroccan lines, but the plan did not survive the first blasts of the guns. The stampede changed direction as soon as the flashes of light, stings of bullets, and gouts of smoke erupted in the cattle's faces. They ran straight back into the ranks of the Songhay. This broke up the Songhay lines and exposed the infantry, who had been massed behind the cattle, to enemy fire. The cavalry, also outmatched by the gunpowder weaponry they faced, were soon forced into retreat. Ishaq II was willing to continue the fight until the bitter end, but one of his advisers told him he would have to answer to God for each of his men who died in the debacle. The army fled.

The Moroccan army captured Gao in the aftermath of Tondibi, but when it sacked the city, it was sorely disappointed by its lack of gold. It was obvious that they would have to continue on to the more valuable trading cities, such as Timbuktu. There they found plenty of valuable commodities and also one of the great centres of scholarship in the Islamic world. It did not survive for long.

The scholars who had made Timbuktu famous were banished when they opposed the new rulers of the city.

Though some drifted back, many never returned to their vast abandoned libraries. Some found themselves sold into slavery, never to return to their home.

BEASTLY BATTLES

The use of animals in battle has been common throughout history. Elephants have been popular for their brute strength and the terror they spread through an army. Other animals have been employed in stranger ways – from pigs covered in flaming pitch and driven into the enemy, to beehives dropped on besiegers outside a city's walls.

The conquest of the Songhay did not profit the Moroccan sultan for long. It proved far harder to control the empire than it had been to conquer it, and his army contained many mercenaries who fought only for pay. As the Moroccans withdrew, the former empire was shattered into many small and competing kingdoms. Rarely has a stampede going the wrong way caused such drastic changes to history.

THE WANGGONGCHANG EXPLOSION

· ·

All was well in the Forbidden City palace of Beijing as people got to work on the morning of 30 May 1626. The Tianqi Emperor was being tended to by his eunuchs and, as was usual for the unscholarly ruler, was probably most concerned to turn to the carpentry projects that filled most of his days. Yes, there were rumblings of rebellion in wider China, but his chief officials would take care of them. The emperor sat down for his morning meal.

At around 10 a.m., however, there was more than a rumble. According to a contemporaneous account in the official gazette of the city, a mighty roar and flash of light exploded out of the clear blue sky. A rush of smoke stabbed upwards, and the ground rocked as if the Earth had turned to liquid. Houses shook, and people were knocked off their feet. In a panic, the emperor fled from his dining hall, but, such was the fright that this sudden shock had caused, only one of his retainers followed him. Nowhere in Beijing was truly safe. As they ran, a tile slipped from the palace roof and struck the loyal follower on the head, killing him instantly. From the walls of the Forbidden City, the scale of the devastation would have been obvious.

Over 2 sq. km (0.75 sq. miles) of the city of Beijing had simply been obliterated, and the streets were impassable. Across the city, debris rained from the heavens, and a large stone statue weighing several tonnes was hurled over the city walls. Trees that had stood for centuries were knocked down, their roots left dangling in mid-air. Those who approached the pitiful crying they could hear coming from the rubble were met by stunned victims emerging from the dust as white as ghosts.

Reports soon emerged of just how terrible this calamity had been. A schoolmaster and all of his students, standing in the road one moment, disappeared forever when the blast struck. The imperial elephant house collapsed and the terrified beasts ran amok in the city. A man was bowing gracefully to some people he had met in the street but before he could rise a piece of debris had whistled past and taken his head clean off. Many officials who helped run the empire were lost when their houses fell down on top of them. The coffin builders of the city did a roaring trade as people stopped in to buy dozens of coffins at a time to bury their dead relatives.

In all, as many as twenty thousand people may have died in the disaster. Among the most mourned was the young son and heir of the emperor.

The centre of the damage was focused on the

Wanggongchang Armoury, where large amounts of gunpowder were produced for the use of the emperor's armies. It also served as a storage point for several tonnes of explosive powder. This gunpowder was needed because several troubling groups of rebels were threatening imperial power, and potential revolutions could cast down the Ming dynasty.

Blame for the explosion immediately fell on the Wanggongchang Armoury. Something must have ignited the stores of gunpowder there to trigger one of the worst industrial explosions in history. Some suspected sabotage by the emperor's enemies. The Chinese had centuries of experience working with gunpowder and knew the dangers of accidental ignition, but even with the utmost precautions it was never a safe substance.

Others turned to less naturalistic explanations for the calamity. The Chinese emperor was said to rule with the mandate of heaven and if a disaster such as this had befallen him then it could only be meant as a rebuke from the gods for some failure of piety. The emperor ordered all of his officials to don mourning clothes and spend time in introspection to search out any moral causes of the explosion. He himself would undertake purifying rituals and offer a sacrifice to the imperial ancestors. Money was lavished on the rebuilding of the city, which the barely adequate imperial treasury could ill afford as it needed to support the loyalty of the armies.

COSMIC CAUSES?

While contemporary sources blame the gunpowder factory, the cause of the Wanggongchang explosion has been hotly debated. Some have attributed the disaster to an earthquake. Others have suggested causes ranging from volcanic eruptions to a meteorite exploding over the city.

These acts of filial piety do not seem to have helped win the blessing of heaven, as the Tianqi Emperor died just one year later. As his only son had died, the throne passed to a younger brother. The new Chongzhen Emperor used his position to remove the powerful imperial eunuchs he thought had given his brother poor advice, and the sudden change in government further destabilized the regime. The Chongzhen Emperor was to be the last of the famed Ming dynasty.

Peasant rebellions broke out against the corruption of the new officials. Manchu forces, continually harassing the northern border, soon invaded. The poverty of the imperial throne weakened support for it, as troops went underpaid and underfed. When faced by the armies of the Manchu, many towns and forts surrendered without a fight. In 1644, the emperor was forced to flee from Beijing and, unable to see any way of recovering the situation, took his own life. The Manchu ruler Hong Taiji took the throne as the first emperor of the Qing dynasty, which ruled the country for the next four hundred years.

Without the Wanggongchang explosion undermining Ming power in the capital and robbing the emperor of his heir, it is possible that the dynasty might have ruled far longer. There is no doubt that the failure to move the production of such a dangerous substance outside of the capital hastened the Ming's demise.

Part III

THE MODERN WORLD

DUTCH TULIP MANIA COSTS MILLIONS

· ·

The sixteenth century in Europe was not only a time of religious and social revolution but also a botanical one. The overseas empires of many nations sent back seeds and plants that had never been seen before in the Old World. A European could dine on potatoes, cultivate tomatoes for their beauty (they were initially thought to be poisonous) and take chocolate as a medicine, none of which had been known to their ancestors.

Alongside the transportation of food crops came a desire to own rare and exquisite blooms. While a large and manicured garden was the preserve of only the very wealthiest of the nobility, most householders with a green thumb could find a patch of soil to tend a few examples of exotic plants. It was always exciting when a new variety of plant arrived from abroad, and connoisseurs of botany competed to own the most beautiful blossoms. It was in this heightened fashion for flowers that the tulip arrived in Northern Europe from Turkey.

The tulip, which we can easily buy today for a low cost, was a sensation when it reached Vienna in the baggage of an ambassador. The bulbs and seeds were sent on to the Low Countries, where they were bred to withstand the less sunny weather of the north. Tulips arrived in the Golden Age of the Dutch Republic, when greater numbers of people shared more prosperity than ever before and were looking for ways to spend their cash.

By the 1630s, the Dutch Republic was one of the wealthiest nations in Europe, thanks to its position at the hub of trade that stretched from the Baltic all the way to the spice islands of the Pacific Ocean. The wealth generated by a single successful voyage could make a person rich for life, but the cost of outfitting a ship was generally prohibitive. Joint stock ventures allowed people to pool their resources to go into business and each reap the rewards of their investment while also sharing the risks of loss. In a very short time, the Dutch had developed many of the systems, such as stock markets, that continue to drive the global economy. People became used to investing and making large returns as the markets boomed, spending their wealth on land, art and other signifiers of success. The tulip was adopted as one such sign of affluence.

Tulips became a highly sought-after commodity for the rich, who competed to have the best and most vibrant varieties. Breeders of tulips crossed known types to generate new varieties to enchant buyers. Plain flowers of a single colour were the most common, but ones with streaks of white and other colours mixed in were quickly developed. The ultimate tulips were those with desirable colours in a flame pattern on each petal. The tulip breeders were masters of promotion and gave their creations pompous names, such as General of Generals, or Semper Augustus.

The tulip trade became one of the most profitable around, as the cultivation of the flowers was relatively simple but the bulbs could sell for large sums. Traders met in taverns to haggle over the bulbs on offer, which they could then trade with other people for greater sums. A sought-after bulb might change hands several times before it was ever planted.

There was one flaw in the tulip trade, which was that tulips only flower for a relatively brief time each year. When you bought a bulb, you took it on trust that it would produce the bloom that was promised. Tulip trading was a speculative market, and people rapidly began to trade not the bulbs themselves but contracts that promised tulip bulbs would be delivered at some specified time in the future. The pieces of paper were as good as the bulbs, so more buyers rushed in to purchase them. This was one of the first market booms ever recorded.

When tulip mania, as this mad enthusiasm for tulips is known, was in full swing in 1636, a single bulb is said to have been auctioned for as much money as it would cost to buy a fashionable house in Amsterdam. A bulb might change hands for as much as a skilled worker made in a decade. At the end of 1636, the prices for tulip contracts doubled, and then doubled again. It seemed as if everyone was about to get rich, but markets are fickle beasts. People began to suspect that the pieces of paper, or the bulbs they represented, were hugely overvalued. Auctioneers became unable to sell tulips despite repeatedly slashing their prices, so that by the summer of 1637, the mania was over and tulips were just another flower, sold like any other in the marketplace.

EATING TULIPS

During the last years of the Second World War, many Dutch people facing food scarcity turned to eating tulip bulbs. Recipes for everything from tulip soup to bread made with tulip flour were published to help stave off starvation.

Those left holding the bulbs at the end of this had at least the promise of some nice bouquets, but those who had invested large sums in contracts were often left with nothing. Many people must have lost fortunes with the contraction of the tulip market. While the collapse of tulip mania had little effect on the Dutch economy as a whole, it was the first sharp lesson on the dangers of the unlimited free market.

The madness of the tulip bubble was understood at the time. A painting titled Wagon of Fools by Hendrik Gerritsz Pot, painted in 1640, shows Flora, the goddess of flowers, riding in a rickety cart with a host of personified vices, all clutching tulips. In their wake march people drawn away from their usual labours to invest in tulips. The message was clear – markets can go down as well as up, and only fools trust in them.

The Darien Scheme Fails

The 1690s were a bad time for Scotland. The coldest years for centuries had hampered crop production and driven the population into decline. Though it was a sovereign nation, it shared its monarch with England, its more prosperous neighbour to the south. For many, it seemed as though England was slowly strangling Scotland, as ever more money poured into that country from its trade and empire while Scotland became a stagnating backwater. A few Scots suggested that Scotland should simply form a union with England so that they could reap some of the benefits of empire, but more Scots resisted this affront to their national pride.

It was during these tough times that a daring project was envisaged that would catapult Scotland into the league of European nations with profitable colonies. The Scottish parliament created the Company of Scotland, which was granted a monopoly on Scottish trade with America, India and Africa, in hopes of changing Scotland's fortunes. Investors piled in to raise money for the company, and all expected great returns on their shares – they just needed the right scheme to back.

William Paterson, a Scot who had travelled to the Caribbean as a young man, became convinced that there was a way to make a fortune there. The plan he developed was to set up a colony on the isthmus of Panama, where only a short stretch of land called the Darien Gap separated the Atlantic from the Pacific Ocean. Goods from the East could be carried overland and then shipped back to Europe. This would open up an entirely new route for trade, and the colony would welcome ships from all nations, with the Company earning a percentage of everything that came through it. Paterson suggested his Darien scheme to the Company of Scotland and found many enthusiastic backers.

When it was announced that the Darien scheme needed volunteers to help construct the new colony, hundreds leapt at the opportunity for what seemed like a grand adventure and rich rewards. In July 1698, ships crammed with one thousand two hundred colonists departed from Scotland for a new life. Many of these people were left buried in paupers' graves far from their homes.

The first sign that things would not be as glorious as many of the colonists had been promised was that they were held below decks for much of the three-month voyage. Filth and disease were widespread, but, remarkably, only seventy colonists died on the journey. It must have been with some relief that they landed in Darien in November and began the building of their new home, which they called Caledonia.

The first order of business was to set up a fort to protect what they hoped would be a valuable new colony. Despite the promise of easy land for the taking, the colonists wasted two months trying to build on what turned out to be a swamp, so they had to try a new location. They found more solid ground and made their fort there, but they had picked another inhospitable spot where agriculture was difficult. Part of the scheme had been to trade with the indigenous population for food until the colony was established, but the locals were not interested in the Western goods the colonists had to offer, so no food was forthcoming.

Things became even worse when the tropical rains started and washed away much of the progress that had been made in founding the colony. The warm and damp environment did not aid crops but did make a fertile breeding ground for diseases. William Paterson had brought his wife and child with him on this adventure, and both ended up in graves in his colony. Hundreds of other colonists weakened by hunger followed them into the ground, while many more were left unfit for any work through disease. Food had to be rationed, and what little was on offer was made mouldy by the conditions. One surviving colonist, Richard Oswald, recalled having a small amount of flour to last a whole week, and before even that could have been eaten, it had to be boiled to kill the 'big maggots and worms' that lived in it. As desperation grew, it became policy that only those who did manual labour could claim a ration – if you fell sick, you starved.

What Paterson and the others in charge had not expected was that other nations would not be happy to have a new neighbour. The Spanish, in particular, did not welcome anyone who might threaten the routes taken by their silver fleets. The English court issued orders that forbade English ships to trade with the Scottish colonists, for fear of rousing Spanish anger. Word reached Caledonia that a force of Spanish ships had been dispatched to attack the colony, and it was decided that the only option was to abandon the scheme. The struggling survivors of Caledonia boarded their ships and sailed away in hopes of safety.

JUDGEMENT OF HISTORY

When Thomas Babington Macaulay wrote his history of England in the nineteenth century, he included one of the most savage judgements ever penned by a historian on the Darien scheme. 'The story is an exciting one… [but] it may well be doubted whether, even now, after the lapse of more than a century and a half, feelings hardly compatible with temperate examination will not be stirred up in many minds by the name of Darien. In truth that name is associated with calamities so cruel that the recollection of them may not unnaturally disturb the equipoise even of a fair and sedate mind.'

That was not the end of Caledonia, however, as a second fleet of settlers had already departed from Scotland in total ignorance of the disaster unfolding there. After their own rough crossing, the colonists arrived to find only ruined huts and hundreds of graves. This alarmed some, but the leaders insisted on rebuilding the fort in preparation for an assault by the Spanish that they learned was being mustered. The Spanish laid siege to the fort and closed off the harbour for a month before pestilence and hunger forced the Scots to surrender and depart. Of the thousands who had sailed to Caledonia, only a few hundred ever straggled back to Scotland.

Many lost their lives in this debacle, but thousands more at home lost their life savings. Around 10 per cent of all the money available in Scotland had been invested in the Company, and now it was all squandered. Paterson, the chief pusher of the Darien scheme that was supposed to rescue Scotland, now became one of the loudest supporters of union with England if it would help pay off the national debt. In 1707, an Act of Parliament created the Kingdom of Great Britain from the union of England and Scotland. The failure of the Darien scheme can be directly linked to the end of Scotland as a sovereign power.

BRITAIN TAXES ITS COLONIES
AND PROVOKES WAR

· ·

The American Revolutionary War is often framed as one of downtrodden and plucky American colonists against the harsh and tyrannical rule of the despotic King George III of Great Britain. At stake, it is claimed, was the very notion of liberty for millions of Americans. In fact, it was, at heart, a tax revolt that was allowed to get out of hand.

By the 1750s, Britain had colonized much of the North American continent and many of the islands of the Caribbean, reaping huge financial rewards from their trade. While having an empire can be financially rewarding, holding on to it can come with huge costs. To defend the land it had taken, the British government found itself having to send navies and armies thousands of kilometres to fend off rival states with an eye to territorial expansion.

In 1754, the French and Indian War broke out as France began to construct forts in the Ohio River valley, which the British colonies considered theirs. At first, the disorganized colonial militias suffered many setbacks against the French and their allies among the indigenous peoples. This changed when William Pitt came to power in Great Britain and war was officially declared between Britain and France, marking the beginning of the Seven Years War. To fight this war, Pitt borrowed heavily and used the money raised to finance campaigns that saw the French and their Spanish allies pushed back all over the globe. At the Treaty of Paris in 1763, Great Britain was granted the French colony of Canada, vast swathes of the Mississippi Valley from France and Florida from Spain. It was a great victory for the British, but a costly one.

Britain's national debt had nearly doubled in the course of the war, and the costs of holding onto all of its new lands would have to be borne by the government. The American economy had boomed during the war, as merchants profited from trading the supplies needed to maintain armies. With the war over, this market dried up, and many were left with debt. Many Americans, who at this point considered themselves just as British as those who had been born and raised in Britain itself, thought they had already paid enough for the defence of their lands and should not be asked to contribute any further. Benjamin Franklin calculated that millions of pounds had been spent by the colonists during the war.

To help defray the costs incurred during the war, the British Parliament enacted the Stamp Act in 1765. This required that many printed works could only be produced using paper embossed with an official symbol, and this paper could only be bought from Britain using British pounds. In the colonies, whenever a legal document was written, a newspaper was read, or a game of cards was played, it supported the British treasury.

For the British, this was a simple and easy way to raise some much-needed money. Such acts brought in large sums when used in England, so they were not considered unusual when applied to the colonies. However, the Stamp Act was deeply unpopular in America, and a number of committees were formed to challenge its imposition and to send representation to the British government about its perceived unfairness. The government met with American delegates and asked for alternative ways to bring in tax revenue, but none of the colonists had any ready suggestions.

In the colonies, voices were raised against the tax and the very idea of taxes imposed by the British Parliament. Samuel Adams of Boston gave explicit reasons for hating the Stamp Act when he foresaw a time in which taxes on all manner of things might be levied on the colonies, even though they had no part in making the laws that established the taxes. Alexander Hamilton wondered how long it would be before every knife, fork, table and chair would be taxed. 'No taxation without representation' became a rallying cry for those who opposed the Stamp Act. Pamphlets decrying it were distributed, and in many colonies, people took to the streets. All were outraged that their rights as natural-born Englishmen were being trampled on.

This attitude rather puzzled members of Parliament in London. While Britain was a democracy, it was one in which only males over a certain age and holding a certain amount of property could cast their vote. Millions of British men, not to mention all women, had no say in which laws were passed and did not rise up in revolt every time a tax was imposed. Parliament held that such unenfranchised people were virtually represented, and that the American colonists were no different. Besides, they said, the American colonists were taxed at a lower rate than British subjects living at home. Given the outpouring of feeling against the act, Parliament did rescind the law in 1766 – but still insisted on its right to tax British subjects wherever they lived.

More laws soon followed, which saw the British government tax everything from glass to paint to tea in an effort to raise money from its colonies. The rates of taxation were kept low, but many American thinkers told colonists to resist even these small impositions, to avoid creating a precedent for further taxation. People in the colonies were encouraged to boycott British goods, to deny any income to the British Crown.

Faced with restive colonies, the British sent troops to ensure order was kept in many ports and cities, and insisted that the soldiers be quartered in American homes at American expense. In 1770, blood was spilled in Boston when British troops opened fire on a mob surrounding them and killed five people.

Thirteen of the American colonies began to band together and form a congress that, at first, sought to petition King George III for redress for their grievances. These were rebuffed by a British government that considered its position to be supreme when it came to the imposition of laws and tariffs. When the army was commanded to disarm the colonial militias, fighting broke out in earnest. In 1776, Congress issued the Declaration of Independence, which dissolved the union between the colonies, now states, and Great Britain. By the end of the American War of Independence, Britain had lost all of its holdings in North America, except for Canada and the Caribbean, all for the sake of a few pennies on the price of a pound of tea.

BOSTON TEA PARTY

In 1773, a group known as the Sons of Liberty dressed as native Americans and boarded three ships in Boston harbour that were carrying British tea. They gathered the three hundred chests of tea in their holds and dumped them into the harbour, to prevent them from being sold. This attack on British trade became known as the Boston Tea Party, even though it was far from a pleasant afternoon affair.

THE FLIGHT TO VARENNES DOOMS THE FRENCH KING

The American Revolution succeeded in driving out British government control from thirteen of its former colonies in North America, relying heavily on France for aid in their struggle. The French had seen the revolution as a tempting way of bloodying the nose of the British Empire and weakening it by removing some of its most prosperous colonies. France had sent men and materiel to North America and fought the

British around the globe. The last battle of the Revolutionary War was actually fought between British and French ships off the coast of India.

Despite the ultimate victory of the American colonies when the peace treaties were signed at the end of the war, France found that it had actually gained very little for its involvement. Despite spending over a billion *livres*, the French found themselves with only some extra fishing rights in Newfoundland when the dust settled. This money had to be recouped somehow, so taxes were raised on subjects in France.

Taxes in France were paid not by everyone but just by the common people, as the clergy and nobility were exempted from most exactions. In fact, when one minister suggested that everyone should pay something this time, his effigy was burned throughout France, and he was forced to go into exile. The French king Louis XVI was used to living in splendour and had to spend huge sums to keep his court and hangers-on in the manner to which they had become accustomed, so the income from tax was desperately needed. As the common people began to grumble at the amounts being asked of them, the nobility at Versailles continued to feast and party.

The American Revolution that France had done so much to support was a signal to the world that it was possible to overthrow rule by a monarch, no matter how mighty they appeared. This notion suddenly began to look very appealing to some French thinkers, who chafed under the near absolute authority of the French Crown.

The exact causes of the French Revolution are hotly debated, and the political manoeuvring too complex to trace in detail, but in 1789, a mob stormed the Bastille. The outbreak of violence was followed by crowds storming Versailles and the French royal family becoming virtual prisoners in the Tuileries palace in Paris. The revolution started to become more extreme, with ever greater declarations of liberty, equality and brotherhood.

Other monarchs looked on in horror at the events in France. If the French throne, one of the oldest and most powerful in Europe, could be toppled, then no king or queen could consider themselves safe. Revolution was an infectious disease. Foreign courts received ambassadors from Louis XVI, asking for their assistance in putting down the forces ranged against him by his own people. If this had been discovered, the revolutionaries would have considered Louis to be a traitor.

With help not immediately at hand, the king decided to free himself from the rabble who now controlled his movements and administration. A plot was hatched to smuggle the king, his queen (Marie Antoinette), and his family out of the Tuileries and get them to a castle that was still loyal to the royalist cause, some 350 km (217 miles) away in Montmédy. From there, it was hoped that Louis could lead forces to put down the revolution. They could also be escorted from there across the border into Austria, under the protection of the queen's brother, Emperor Joseph II.

On the night of 20 June 1791, the royal family crammed into a large and ostentatious coach drawn by six horses and began to trundle away from the palace. Advisers had suggested using two light coaches that could move more swiftly and avoid detection, but the king and queen insisted on keeping the family together. The king left a written declaration behind that repudiated many of the concessions he had been forced to make before, to rub salt in the wounds of his revolutionary captors.

The royal party was fairly conspicuous but nevertheless managed to escape the capital. They had planned to pretend to be servants of an invented Russian noble lady if they were questioned, but the disguise did not last long. The king gave out money and silver plate to those who helped him along the route, and many people recognized their monarch. The escape was also slowed when the royal coach broke a wheel and had to be repaired. This delay meant they failed to meet up with a company of soldiers who would have guarded them, whose commander panicked and fled when the royal party did not reach him on schedule.

In Paris, the flight from the palace had been discovered, and parties were sent out to hunt for the absconded monarch. They got a firm lead when a postmaster spotted the similarity between the disguised king and a portrait on a bank note in his pocket. He raced to the town of Varennes to inform the authorities there that the royal family was fleeing in their direction. It was in Varennes that the king was apprehended and sent back to Paris under guard.

AXEL VON FERSEN'S AFFAIRS

Count von Fersen was a Swedish nobleman who had seen action in the American War of Independence and was a close intimate of Marie Antoinette – some have suggested the two were lovers. It was von Fersen who engineered the flight to Varennes. Once it failed, he returned to politics in Sweden, where, in 1810, he was beaten to death by a mob.

The Paris mob was furious that their king had tried to run away from them. They were more angered that he appeared to have appealed to a foreign power for help in suppressing their rights. The voices who had called for Louis to become a mere constitutional monarch were replaced by those calling for the complete abolition of the monarchy itself. The political landscape became shattered by the flight to Varennes, as this escapade became known, and the king's support dwindled.

With Austria preparing to invade France in support of King Louis, the increasingly radical leaders of the revolution put the former ruler on trial for treason. In 1793, he was found guilty and executed publicly on the guillotine. Marie Antoinette followed him to her death nine months later. Had the flight to Varennes succeeded, who knows what course much of French, European and world history might have taken.

NAPOLEON INVADES RUSSIA AND DESTROYS HIS OWN EMPIRE

. . . .

In the tumult of the French Revolution, one man rose from almost nothing to the extremes of political power. Napoleon Bonaparte was an unlikely ruler of France since he came from Corsica, an island that had only been in French hands for a year when he was born, and spoke Corsican Italian as a child. The revolutionary attitude of radical equality opened up careers that had once been the preserve of titled gentlemen to anyone who showed the requisite ability, and Napoleon was nothing if not talented.

Within a few short years of graduating from military academy, Napoleon's skills were being used to defend the revolutionary government from its enemies, both foreign and domestic. He was given command of the French army in Italy and, in a series of stunning victories, defeated the Austrian Empire. It was as a military genius that Napoleon came to take the position of First Consul of the French Republic, and eventually had himself crowned as Emperor Napoleon.

Other European monarchs banded together, with the backing of Britain, to attempt to quell this upstart empire, but somehow Napoleon kept winning battles and expanding his domain. At the height of its power in 1812, the French Empire stretched from the Atlantic Ocean in Spain to the borders of Russia. Many of the states Napoleon conquered were held as client states tied to him by treaty, but Napoleon was not averse to doling out lands to his family. His brother Joseph was made first King of Naples and Sicily and then King of Spain. It seemed as though the future of Europe lay in the hands of the Bonapartes.

One does not place an imperial crown on one's head without a lofty sense of one's ability, and Napoleon seems to have come to believe he was invincible. In 1812, the Russian Tsar Alexander I told Napoleon to withdraw French troops from the lands bordering Russia, but instead of agreeing, the French emperor declared war. With an eye for detail, he drew up his plans for an invasion that included nearly half a million troops and auxiliary support staff. Tens of thousands of horses and wagons set off towards the Russian frontier, and his men marched in full confidence that this would be another of Napoleon's strategic masterstrokes.

It is not possible here to detail all of the movements of the *Grande Armée*, as the French force was known, but after several unusually bloody battles, Napoleon marched into Moscow in September. The Russians had burned crops in the fields to deny food to their foe, and they retreated to deny them a decisive confrontation. Napoleon settled in to wait for the tsar to come and negotiate a peace. His assumption was that the Russians would not tolerate their capital being in French hands. He was right in a sense – just days after the occupation began, Russian agents set fire to much of the city, so that Napoleon was king of a heap of ashes.

Instead of marching onwards to force a battle, or home towards safety, Napoleon decided to overwinter in Moscow. Napoleon's former energy and genius for capturing the advantage of a situation seem to have deserted him at this moment. Messages were sent to the tsar, but Alexander never deigned to reply to Napoleon. Alexander I knew he could wait Napoleon out as the tsar had the harsh Russian winter on his side.

The French were poorly supplied in Moscow. The long lines of communication back to French territory were vulnerable to attack, and supplies could not quickly be sent along them. Cossack fighters would attack French soldiers sent out to forage, and the Russian peasants also defended what little they had from plunder: the French would starve if they stayed in Moscow. Then the snow began to fall. Even Napoleon had to recognize that a disaster was brewing – he ordered a retreat from the city.

Napoleon left Moscow behind him in flames, but that heat would not warm his men for long. His plan had been to leave Russia by a different route, via lands that had not already been ransacked, but the Russian forces who shadowed the retreat kept him in despoiled territory. There was not even enough fodder for the horses that officers rode or that pulled wagons, so when the army passed a house with a thatched roof, they would strip it to give something to their mounts. This was insufficient, however, and horse corpses soon littered the road. More horses died of cold or slipped on the ice as the weather became ever more frigid. The heavy cannons that Napoleon had employed so brilliantly in his rise to power had to be abandoned, for want of beasts to drag them.

The men suffered equally. It was so cold that many found their guns welded to their hands by the frost. Those who fell asleep never rose. Comrades stopped helping one another because they did not even have the strength to reach down and help another to stand up. Anyone who managed to start a fire would find themselves shoved aside into the snow as others rushed forward for a moment of warmth.

On 5 December, Napoleon fatefully decided to escape from the remnants of what had once been the grandest army in Europe. In a sled, he sped away from the straggling body of soldiers who had followed him so far

from home. The common men of the *Grande Armée* had no such opportunity for escape.

THE BATTLE OF THE BUNNIES

While Napoleon was thought to be almost unbeatable in battle before the invasion of Russia, he had suffered one humiliating loss, in 1807. He had ordered rabbits to be gathered for a celebratory hunt, but when the hundreds of caged animals were released, instead of fleeing the guns, they all swarmed Napoleon. The emperor was forced to retreat to his carriage in the face of a wave of rabbits.

It is not possible to place an exact figure on how many French died in this single campaign, but just over a hundred thousand of the five hundred thousand who set out ever managed to reach their homes again. It was a shattering defeat for the unconquerable Napoleon and left him with a severe shortage of recruits to rebuild his forces. The War of the Sixth Coalition saw Britain, Russia, Austria, Spain and Prussia attack the weakened empire in 1813. Napoleon, who had once held Europe in his grip, was forced to abdicate in

1814 and was sent into exile on the island of Elba. Despite a heroic effort to retake his throne in 1815, his hopes of a return to glory were dashed on the battlefield of Waterloo, and Napoleon was sent to wander the tiny and isolated island of St Helena for the rest of his days.

DARWIN DROPS OUT OF MEDICAL SCHOOL

· ·

Many stories are told of people who drop out of university to follow their dreams and end up becoming outstanding in their field. Such tales usually involve business or artistic endeavours; it is rare for a scientist to have made a world-changing contribution after failing to get a degree. For the history of science, though, it was probably a good thing that Charles Darwin gave up on his university studies.

Charles Darwin was born in 1809 to a family of medical doctors. His father Robert had been a doctor, and his grandfather Erasmus had, too. Both had studied at the medical school in Edinburgh, then the best in the world, and it was natural that Charles and his brother would also be sent there. Darwin's father had low expectations for Charles and told the young man that he would disgrace the family, since he cared for nothing but shooting and rat-catching. Despite this, the Darwin brothers began their studies in 1825.

It soon became apparent that Charles was not suited to a life of medicine, as he found the surgeries he witnessed to be hugely distressing. In that time before anaesthesia, surgeries were accompanied by a symphony of screaming and thrashing. Darwin was sickened by the blood and pain and, writing his autobiography years later, was still traumatized by the things he witnessed.

I also attended on two occasions the operating theatre in the hospital at Edinburgh, and saw two very bad operations, one on a child, but I rushed away before they were completed. Nor did I ever attend again, for hardly any inducement would have been strong enough to make me do so; this being long before the blessed days of chloroform. The two cases fairly haunted me for many a long year.

The lecturers in medicine were equally distasteful to Darwin. He described Dr Alexander Munro's lectures on human anatomy as being as dull as the doctor himself. Indeed, Darwin thought that he could learn just as much by reading as he did at lectures.

There may have been another reason that Darwin did

not care for medicine as it was taught at Edinburgh. To be granted a licence to practise by the College of Physicians, the students had to perform several dissections of a human body. Unfortunately, there were never enough cadavers to go around, since only the bodies of executed criminals were supposed to be used.

The medical schools therefore turned to the 'resurrection men' to supply the rest. These men would head out to graveyards and dig up any recently interred corpses to sell them to students and schools for use in dissections. Darwin must have been aware of how the bodies he studied were being procured, which no doubt provoked a little squeamishness. In 1828, William Burke and William Hare decided that digging up corpses was too much bother and began murdering people to sell them to the school. When this was discovered, questions were asked about just how culpable the medical school should be found in buying these bodies.

After a short period, Darwin's brother decided to leave Edinburgh to study medicine in London. Charles was left alone without his closest companion, studying something in which he had no interest. There were opportunities to pursue other research in a university town, however. In his second year, Darwin joined the Plinian Society, where he found a group of young students willing to discuss the most radical notions of biology, including some who held that all of the biological world could be explained in a materialist way, without reference to God.

Darwin's time was spent studying zoological matters and collecting samples of marine life from the nearby Firth of Forth. He made his first scientific discoveries by examining the microscopic creatures he dredged up there. Eventually, it became clear to Darwin's father, who had been bankrolling this education, that there was no hope of Charles becoming a respectable doctor. In 1827, Darwin withdrew from Edinburgh without gaining a degree.

This might have been the end of Darwin as far as science went. He might have just become a country gentleman who did a little scientific dabbling, but Darwin's father had other ideas. He shipped Charles off to Cambridge to fulfil the studies needed to become a clergyman.

TRAINING IN TAXIDERMY

While in Edinburgh, Darwin studied the art of animal taxidermy under John Edmonstone, a freed slave. Edmonstone's techniques would later be used to preserve Darwin's specimens that he collected around the globe.

Once again, Darwin found his interests directed elsewhere. He became a keen beetle hunter, intensely interested in how the samples he collected were related to each other. At Edinburgh he had learned about the scientist Jean-Baptiste Lamarck's theory of evolution and was reminded of his own grandfather's ideas on how species came to exist. It was in meeting and learning from naturalists at Cambridge that Darwin came to accept that he was not cut out for the priesthood. After four years of university, he left Cambridge with a degree but no clear goal in life. He had, however, become a great friend of the botany professor John Stevens Henslow.

It was Henslow who put Darwin's name forward to join an expedition being planned for the HMS *Beagle*. The captain of the Beagle wanted a gentleman companion for the long voyage who could also act as the ship's naturalist, so Darwin, a pleasant person to spend several months with, was taken on board. The things Darwin saw on this voyage started his train of thought leading to the theory of evolution by natural selection that made him world famous, and changed the intellectual landscape of the entire world.

GENERAL D. H. HILL LOSES SPECIAL ORDER 191

Civil wars are among the most uncivil of all conflicts, and the American Civil War of 1861 to 1865 was no exception. The Union forces of the north, under the command of President Lincoln, faced the breakaway states of the South, who fought as the Confederacy. The Union was fighting to preserve the unity of the United States, while the South claimed to be fighting for independence from a central government that was trampling on their rights – specifically, the right to hold black people in bondage as slaves. As the war progressed, each side came to believe the worst of the other, so fighting was brutal and campaigns claimed hundreds of thousands of lives.

In 1862, the Confederate army under General Robert E. Lee was preparing to strike northwards in an invasion of Union territory. Should they capture and sack Washington, D.C., the capital of the United States, it might be a decisive stroke to tip the war in their favour. A Union army under George B. McClellan was charged with seeing to the defence of Washington, but McClellan, notoriously cautious and seeming to believe that the Confederate army was vastly more numerous than it was in reality, was a controversial choice for this role. When the Confederates did strike into Maryland, however, it was McClellan who would have to stop them.

General Lee was meticulous in the planning of his march into the north and knew McClellan well. Lee's efforts involved splitting his force into smaller units that would attack and capture strategic points, including Harper's Ferry, where John Brown had once tried to raise a slave rebellion. If this plan worked, his forces would have strong defensive positions and access to large supplies needed for the campaign to come. It is always dangerous for an army to break up in this way, but Lee gambled that McClellan would not trust in the forces under his own command and so be slow to react.

Lee issued his commands to the army in a text known as Special Order 191, which was copied several times and passed out to the various commanders under him. One of these orders was given to General D. H. Hill, who was charged with defending the rear of the Confederate march to assure that supply lines were maintained. It was a copy that was with his force that went astray and changed the course of the war.

Just a few days after the order had been sent out, some Union infantrymen were scouting a campsite that had just been abandoned by General Hill's force days earlier. Corporal Barton W. Mitchell must have thought himself very lucky when he found a package on the ground near a tree, which turned out to be a piece of paper wrapped around some cigars. It was not the tobacco, however, that proved to be valuable. It was soon realized that the paper was a copy of the orders outlining the Confederate invasion sent to General Hill, left carelessly behind.

Within hours the order was in the hands of General McClellan, who immediately recognized its importance. McClellan declared, 'Now I know what to do!' and that if he did not beat Lee with this intelligence, he deserved to be sent home in disgrace. The genuine nature of the captured order was confirmed by a fellow officer who had once worked in a bank used by the person who had copied it, so he knew the signature well.

McClellan moved at once. He sent out scouts to confirm that the Confederate army was really following the movements described in the orders. McClellan was overjoyed to find out how closely Special Order 191 was being put into practice. He crowed in a letter to President Lincoln, 'I think Lee has made a gross mistake and that he will be severely punished for it... I hope for a great success if the plans of the Rebels remain unchanged... I have all the plans of the Rebels and will catch them in their own trap if my men are equal to the emergency.' Meanwhile, Lee had no idea that his plans had been captured by the enemy but was surprised by how rapidly McClellan was able to counter his attacks.

Three days after McClellan had received Special Order 191, the opposing armies met at the battle of South Mountain, where the Confederates held three passes around the mountains against McClellan's advance. The Union army was victorious and drove the Confederates into retreat. General Lee realized that his planned invasion of the north was now totally in doubt. Had McClellan advanced quickly, he could have destroyed Lee's force entirely, but his cautious nature won out, and he allowed Lee to flee.

This skirmish was quickly followed by the Battle of Antietam, where the armies of Lee and McClellan again faced each other, but this time with strong artillery support. It would prove to be the most deadly day of fighting in United States history, leaving over twenty thousand soldiers dead. Despite the cost the battle was essentially a draw, and McClellan did not follow up on his advantages.

HOW WAS IT LOST?

After the war, General Hill claimed that he had only received a single copy of Special Order 191 and that it had remained in his possession. The copy of the order that was lost seems to have been a second one sent to him by another commander – it never reached Hill's hand, and a soldier had used it as a convenient piece of wrapping paper.

The loss of Special Order 191 might have been the failure that led to the destruction of a major part of the Confederate army. Instead, McClellan's failure to push onwards saw Lee's forces survive to carry on the fighting. The Union side did emerge victorious in the end, and the Battle of Antietam saw off Lee's invasion of Maryland. It was also the success that gave President Lincoln the public support needed to promulgate his Emancipation Proclamation, which legally freed all slaves in the states in rebellion.

ALEXANDER GRAHAM BELL MAKES A MISTRANSLATION AND INVENTS THE TELEPHONE

. . . .

The invention of the telephone has changed the world and connected people in a way rivalled only by the development of the internet. Allowing people in different nations to communicate directly made the world seem much smaller at a time when journeys were measured in days, weeks and months. It is, however, a vexed question as to who is actually responsible for the first working telephone. The person most commonly given the title of 'father of the telephone' is Alexander Graham Bell – and his work began with a serious failure.

Bell was born in 1847 in Edinburgh to a family that had, for at least two generations, made their living from their voices. Teaching elocution and studying the mechanics of sound had been the profession of both Bell's father and grandfather, so it is little surprise that Bell would take an interest in transmitting voices.

When Bell was a young man his mother began to lose her hearing, and he developed a method of speaking in a low, bass rumble against her forehead. He realized that the vibrations of his words were able to be conducted through the bone in a way that his mother could interpret. Bell also learned the skill of rendering any sound into a written symbol using his father's universal phonetic alphabet, so that any language represented in this way could be perfectly reproduced, even if he had no knowledge of the language itself.

In 1863, Bell and his brothers witnessed a mechanical man that could be made to speak simple words and phrases. The family was enchanted by this novelty and soon set about attempting to build their own model; they created a lifelike head that, via the manipulation of its lips and windpipe, could be made to speak. Bell became hooked on the idea of recreating a human voice by mechanical means and wrote to an expert about his experiments. The expert suggested that Bell should read the work of the German scientist Hermann von Helmholtz. When Bell set about translating this, it was here that he made his most productive failure.

While reading this book, Bell mistranslated a key passage from Helmholtz's research. Helmholtz suggested that it was possible for the vowel sounds of a language to be reproduced using a series of tuning forks. Bell thought that Helmholtz had actually already done this and transmitted the sounds he wished to create using electrical wiring. Having moved with his family to Canada, living in a cabin with little to do, Bell set about making his own version of the device he wrongly assumed had been made once before. Bell spent so many nights experimenting with his inventions that his mother had to beg him to go to sleep.

Later, Bell would reflect on his mistake, saying, 'I thought that Helmholtz had done it and that my failure was due only to my ignorance of electricity. It was a very valuable blunder. It gave me confidence. If I had been able to read German in those days, I might never have commenced my experiments.'

Bell was living at a time when the electrical telegraph had already revolutionized communications. Using Morse code, written texts could be transmitted at high speed between any locations connected by wires. Bell was thrilled by the invention but also saw its limitations in requiring professionals trained in Morse code to be at both ends of the telegraph and only one message to be sent at any one time. Bell realized that if a device could be constructed that allowed instantaneous speech to be transmitted and received at the same time, it would be possible to have conversations at a distance. He dubbed this putative invention the harmonic telegraph.

The only problem with Bell's idea was that he needed something to capture the voice, a microphone, and something to turn an electrical signal into audible sound, a speaker, and neither device existed. Then, in a chance encounter, Bell met an electrical engineer called Thomas Watson who could help him make his dream a reality, and the two began to collaborate.

In 1875, Bell and Watson made a breakthrough when they discovered that a simple piece of metal vibrating beside a magnet was able to transmit the sound it created electronically along a wire and be heard at the other end by a similar set-up. Soon, the pair were able to hold short conversations using their telephone. In one, probably apocryphal, tale, the first telephone call was Bell asking for Watson to come and help him after spilling battery acid on himself. The true first clearly audible phone message was actually Bell saying, 'Mr Watson, come here, I want to see you.'

Bell rushed to the patent office and was granted U.S. patent 174,465 for his 'Improvement in telegraphy'. He narrowly beat Elisha Gray who was working on a similar telephone, though the two waged legal battles that reached all the way to the Supreme Court before Bell's patent was upheld.

In 1876, Bell debuted his invention at the Centennial Exhibition in Philadelphia. The Emperor of Brazil was present when Bell read some lines of Hamlet into the telephone and was so shocked when the voice was projected at the other end that he squawked, 'My God! It talks!' Within a few years, telephone exchanges were being set up in many major cities that allowed connections between phones to be made in various locations. Bell became a very wealthy man thanks to his invention, which allowed him to spend more time working on other inventions. Had Bell never failed in his German, it is likely someone else would be credited with the invention of the telephone.

AHOY!

It was a vexed question as to how you should greet someone when they answer the telephone. Alexander Graham Bell suggested that the nautical term used to capture someone's attention, 'Ahoy', should be used. In the end, 'Hello' won out instead.

Of course, the telephone has not been an undiluted success – even Bell recognized that having a jangling device that allowed anyone to interrupt you in your own home could sometimes be annoying. He refused to have a telephone in his lab so that he could work undisturbed.

Sloppy Lab Work Leads to Sweet Discoveries

· ·

The brilliant chemist and microbiologist Louis Pasteur once declared that 'Fortune favours the prepared mind.' Careful planning and execution are key to the progress of science, but just as often, the greatest discoveries are made by accident. Ingesting substances in a scientific laboratory is generally the path to a short career and often a shortened life, but sometimes a failure to observe proper lab protocol leads to new insights.

Coal tar is the dark and sticky substance left over when coal is broken down by heat in the production of gas. The faintly noxious substance is composed of over ten thousand different compounds, and it was realized that some of them might have useful properties in the nineteenth century. There was also a lot of coal tar around, as coal was the energy source for much of industry. Scientists love a cheap ingredient.

In 1877, the Russian chemist Constantin Fahlberg was working on chemical reactions involving coal tar, which he found fascinating but of limited commercial value. Being a typically obsessed scientist, however, he would work long hours in the lab trying to find an interesting discovery. One night, he looked at his watch, realized just how late he was working, rushed out for a quick meal to fuel his research, and forgot to wash his hands.

Fahlberg tore into some bread as soon as he sat down and nearly spat it out because it tasted so sweet. He was sure that he had accidentally eaten a piece of cake by mistake, so he rinsed his mouth out. Taking another sip of water, he placed his mouth on the part where his thumb had touched the glass and thought he was drinking syrup. So he sucked the tip of his thumb to check that and discovered that the taste 'out-sugared sugar'. Immediately he knew what had happened – something he was working on in the lab was a new, super-sweet chemical.

Going straight back to the laboratory, Fahlberg tasted the contents of all the beakers on his desk to identify the sweet one. Tasting possibly toxic liquids in the lab is not recommended. Once he found the right compound, Fahlberg set about purifying it and working out how to synthesize it. By getting a patent on his discovery, which he named saccharine, and starting a company to produce it, Fahlberg was able to make his fortune from having dirty hands.

The history of artificial sweeteners has, to a large extent, been shaped by failures of cleanliness. In 1937, a postgraduate student called Michael Sveda was working with medical drugs in the lab and stopped for a moment to have a cigarette, something else not usually permitted in labs these days. When his experiment came to a critical point, he placed his cigarette on the lab bench. After completing his task, he took a puff on his cigarette and found it to be sweet.

Thus, the artificial sweetener cyclamate was discovered. While cyclamates are less sweet than saccharine, they lack its harsh chemical taste. Soon, sweeteners made from a mixture of the two were being sold worldwide, with profits in the billions of dollars. Cyclamate was banned in the United States in 1970 after a study found that rats fed high doses of the sweetener were at a greater risk of developing cancer, but other studies have failed to replicate this link, and it remains available in many countries.

Aspartame is one of the most popular artificial sweeteners available today and can be found in many diet products that offer reduced levels of sugar. Once again, its potential use as an alternative to sugar was discovered thanks to a failure of good lab practice. In 1965 James Schlatter was attempting to synthesize a drug that could help patients who had ulcers. He licked the tip of his finger to riffle through his papers and was startled by the sweet taste.

In a strange case of synchronicity, it was only two years later that another chemist, Karl Clauss, was working in his lab when he too had to pick up a piece of paper. He had accidentally dipped his fingers in a beaker but did not notice until he tasted the sugary compound. That is how the sweetener acesulfame potassium was discovered.

Tate & Lyle is a British company most famous for its sugar, so it is perhaps understandable that they were sponsoring research into the chemistry of sucrose in the 1970s. They were funding chemist Leslie Hough and his student Shashikant Phadnis's studies on the chemicals that could be made from sucrose, to which they had plenty of access. At the time, they were adding chlorine atoms to the compound and observing the results on its chemistry with an eye to potentially using it as an insecticide. The lab had already created a hundred different chlorinated sucrose molecules in search of something useful.

BICYCLE DAY IS A HIGH HOLIDAY

In 1943, Albert Hofmann synthesized lysergic acid diethylamide and touched his face. This momentary contact was enough to spark vivid and fantastical images. So he decided to try a larger dose and bicycled home through the Swiss countryside. After being convinced that the hallucinations he was experiencing would not kill him, Hofmann found himself enjoying his trip. Now 19 April is celebrated annually as Bicycle Day by fans of LSD.

In 1975 Phadnis was told to take one of their creations and 'test' it, but he misheard the instruction as 'taste'. He dipped a small spatula into the substance and placed it on his tongue. Luckily, it was the sweetness of the chemical that overwhelmed him, rather than any toxic side effects. Sucralose, as the compound was dubbed, was utterly useless as an insecticide but did prove very popular as an artificial sweetener.

RUSSIA SELLS ALASKA FOR A PITTANCE

Since the 1840s, some in the United States had begun to dream of a nation that stretched from the Atlantic Ocean to the Pacific across the whole North American continent. The supposed moral superiority of the United States was believed to make it their '*manifest destiny*' to rule this land. Rival claims to this land were not to be heeded, whether they came from the native Americans who already lived there or from other nations.

The United States government was not opposed to purchasing the claims held by other countries when the opportunity presented itself. In 1803, Thomas Jefferson arranged the Louisiana Purchase with France, which doubled the size of his nation at a stroke by buying France's territorial rights to much of the land west of the Mississippi.

British Canada, to the north of the United States, did not seem likely to fall into American hands as easily, but there was another region in North America that might. The Russian Empire had claimed a vast tract of land in the extreme north-west of the continent. Colonization had started in the 1740s when Russian fur traders crossed the Bering Strait in search of valuable hides. The hunters coerced the native population into doing most of the actual fur trapping, while the profits returned to Russia.

Within just a few decades, however, the numbers of sea otters and other lucrative species fell into sharp decline, and each hunting season became less profitable than the last. It was realized in Russia that the small Russian settlements in North America would never be able to hold onto their land should the British seek to take it from them. Then came the Crimean War in 1853, which saw a British, French and Ottoman coalition push Russia to a humiliating defeat, nearly draining them of resources. The Russian holdings in North America were now a costly holdover of imperial dreams and a potential ignition point for another war with Britain.

The solution was to try to sell their territorial claim to the United States to prevent it from falling into British hands. Some Russians also realized that the Americans might eventually take their lands anyway, and there would be nothing they could do to stop it – better to at least profit from a sale than suffer another public display of weakness. Negotiations opened in 1859 but were delayed during the American Civil War – the United States was understandably seeking to reclaim its southern states rather than expand into new territory at the time.

Secretary of State William Seward was deeply in favour of what became known as the Alaska Purchase. Newspaper reports from the time show a generally positive reaction to the United States being enlarged by this means, so long as the price was right. There was also hope that Alaska would be a helpful stepping stone to increasing trade with East Asia.

Not everyone was excited by the chance to own a lot of land with not much in it. The Alaska Purchase was called Seward's Folly; some suggested it would simply be a preserve for polar bears, while others called it Walrussia and Icebergia. Unless something unlikely happened, such as the discovery of major gold deposits, the costs of administering and protecting the new lands would never recoup the initial outlay.

With over 1.5 million square kilometres on offer, the question came down to what a fair exchange would be. The United States offered $7.2 million, which worked out at around $5 per square kilometre. The Russians accepted with alacrity, and the treaty was signed in 1867. Russia was glad to be enriched and rid of a troublesome claim, and the United States was thrilled by the low price they paid. So where is the failure?

The handover of land did not go exactly as planned. A witness to the events at Sitka in Alaska recorded how the Russians ceremonially tried to lower their flag, but it became ensnared on the flagpole. A hardy young soldier sent up to free it found himself repeatedly sliding down the pole. It took two more Russian soldiers to remove the flag before the stars and stripes of the United States could fly over the new territory.

HOME TO MOTHER RUSSIA

The final governor of Russian Alaska bought a sailing ship called *Winged Arrow* to travel home and took with him over a hundred Russian settlers. The crowded ship followed an adventurous course that took in Hawaii, Tahiti and London. Those aboard enjoyed the trip, with widespread drinking whenever they went ashore. One passenger reported that on Tahiti, 'those who were sent ashore to run errands always got drunk and then did not feel like returning, and neither were they in shape to return'.

The population of Alaska soon fell, as Russian settlers returned home and Americans who had ventured there found more promising prospects in less barren locations. Seal-skinning made some a profit, but there remained little in the region to pull in large numbers of settlers. With so much land to explore, there were hopeful prospectors who continued to search for valuable mineral deposits – and in 1896 they found them. There was gold in the Klondike.

Tens of thousands of miners, with nuggets of gold haunting their imaginations, rushed to Alaska the following year. Well over a billion dollars' worth of gold in today's terms was shipped back to the United States. There was so much gold dust floating around and being used as currency that even those sweeping bar-room floors could become rich by pocketing the contents of their pans at the end of an evening. Not only those who found gold made money, but also those who sold them the necessary tools and goods. Ports boomed with activity, and new towns sprang up with infrastructure to support the miners.

The gold rush ended, as they always do, but, later, fields of silver, zinc and oil boosted the economy of Alaska and the wider United States. Beyond the simple resources available from the land, the United States also found that Alaska was vital to strategic defence during the Cold War against the Soviet Union. With Alaska as their 'Guardian of the North', the United States could detect incoming missiles and troop landings. There were many in the Soviet Union who would have loved to have access to North America and regretted the sale for such a paltry amount.

Franz Ferdinand's Driver Takes a Wrong Turn

. . . .

Needless to say, wars are complex affairs with myriad causes. Economic, political and psychological aspects all play their part in pushing two nations towards attacking each other. Identifying any one act as the inciting incident is always a simplification, but certain histories might have turned out very differently indeed if just one little change was made. The events of 28 June 1914 offer a vivid example of one ordinary failure snowballing into war.

Europe in 1914 was a complex web of international alliances between nations that all saw themselves as strong empires that had to maintain their prestige. A unified Germany had disrupted the balance of power that had existed for much of the nineteenth century. Eventually two groups formed, with Russia, France and Britain on one side and Germany, Austria-Hungary and the Ottoman Empire on the other. Each was pledged to support the others in their rival alliances.

The hope was that the threat of war between them was too terrible to contemplate, and an armed confrontation was therefore made impossible. Everyone recognized that the technology of warfare had developed massively since the last widespread European conflicts, and the death toll of a modern war would be unlike anything ever seen before. Many nations were arming themselves, though, as growing nationalism saw countries calling for the return of territories they considered to be rightfully theirs. One wrong move might bring the peace of Europe crashing down into an apocalyptic war.

In 1914, it was decided that Archduke Franz Ferdinand, heir to the Austro-Hungarian throne, would visit Sarajevo. Austria-Hungary was a vast multinational and multi-ethnic empire where many subjects of the emperor were not content, and Russia had been supporting states in the Balkans to break free from their old imperial masters. The Austro-Hungarians decided to hold military manoeuvres in Bosnia, which Franz Ferdinand himself would oversee, as a show of force.

Serbian nationalists believed that Bosnia should be free and that the visit of a royal archduke was unwelcome. Worse was that he would be in Sarajevo on St Vitus' Day, which marked an annual celebration of Serbia's victory over Ottoman forces in 1389. Members of a Serbian nationalist group called the Black Hand decided that Franz Ferdinand would not survive his trip.

The Austro-Hungarian authorities were well aware that there might be some sort of action given the level of feeling in the region, but the security measures taken were insignificant. Archduke Franz Ferdinand and his wife Sophie departed from the train station in an open-topped car to witness the loyal crowds who lined their route. Interspersed in the throng were six assassins armed with pistols and bombs.

As the royal motorcar passed one of the killers, a bomb

was thrown directly at them by Nedeljko Čabrinović. Unfortunately for the assassin, it struck the rear of the car and bounced backwards, where it detonated underneath the car behind it. The royal party sped on. Čabrinović, realizing he had failed, swallowed a cyanide capsule and leapt into the nearby river, but the cyanide had degraded and the river was only a few inches deep in the middle of summer, so Čabrinović survived and was swiftly arrested. The high speed of the cars moving to safety prevented any other attempts from taking place. The assassins slunk back into the city, their plan seemingly a failure.

At the town hall, the unhurt Franz Ferdinand delivered a speech and remarked on the joy most people were expressing that he had mercifully escaped the plot. It was decided that the royal couple would visit the hospital where those who had been wounded by the blast were being treated. They once again got into their car and set off, but their driver, Leopold Lojka, had not been informed of the new route they would be taking. When he took the wrong street, a politician who was also riding in the car told him to turn around. Lojka hit the brakes, and the car stalled as an attempt was made to reverse.

The car came to a stop outside a delicatessen. Just outside was another member of the Black Hand, Gavrilo Princip, armed with a pistol. He was actively waiting for an opportunity to strike but never dreamed it would be delivered to him so perfectly. The failure of Franz Ferdinand's driver gave him his chance. He walked up to the car and fired his gun twice – hitting both the archduke and his wife. They died soon afterwards. Gavrilo Princip was quickly arrested, but his gunshots would have loud reverberations for all of Europe.

NO REGRETS

Gavrilo Princip, who was just nineteen years old when he was put on trial for murder and treason, was too young to face the death penalty under the law. He was held in solitary confinement and lived long enough to see the Great War spread. Despite having fired the gun that started the race to war, Princip was unbothered by his role. Before he died of TB in 1918, he told his doctor that he thought the war was inevitable and that he felt no guilt for what had happened.

Austria-Hungary was outraged by this attack on their royal family and feared it would be followed by more aggressive moves. When they learned that the action had been taken by a Serbian nationalist association, they realized that any plans to attack Serbia directly could have dire consequences because Russia had pledged their support to the Serbians. So Austria-Hungary called on Germany to back them in any action they took – a promise Germany was happy to make.

Diplomatic efforts for mediation between the great powers were made, but so were assurances of support if war was declared. Ultimatums were telegraphed between capitals, and armies mobilized along various frontiers. When Austria-Hungary declared war against Serbia on 28 July 1914 it envisioned a limited war, but instead it triggered the entry into the war of all of Europe: the Great War had begun.

By the time the First World War ended, 20 million people had died. The empires of Germany and Austria-Hungary were dismantled, and the Russian monarchy was overthrown in a revolution that culminated in the creation of the Soviet Union. Did one wrong turn really cause all this? It is impossible to say, but history is made of many such moments that leave us with imponderable 'what ifs'.

Tsar Nicholas II Takes Control and Loses Everything

· ·

The First World War was not the gentlemanly affair many had thought it would be. Both sides assumed it would be a short, sharp clash of armies. German soldiers in 1914 were told they would be home before the leaves fell from the trees, while the British were assured that it would all be over by Christmas. Instead, this war was unlike anything that Europe had ever experienced.

The massive armies that were mobilized found themselves literally bogged down in a quagmire of brutal trench warfare on the Western Front. Defensive abilities outstripped the capability of armies to capture territory as machine guns, artillery and chemical weapons revealed the nature of modern warfare to be a grinding slugfest to see which side ran out of men and materiel first. On the Eastern Front the war was just as hard-fought, but the Germans and Austrians were making deep incursions into Russian territory.

It was not meant to be this way for Tsar Nicholas II of Russia. When he ascended the throne in 1894, he was one of the most powerful monarchs in the world. The court of the Romanov dynasty was almost farcically wealthy, and the princes, princesses, dukes and duchesses who surrounded Nicholas II owned vast tracts of land and wore more diamonds than there were stars in the heavens. Other European rulers looked on with jealousy because the tsar was supreme ruler within his domain and did not have to bother with most of the trappings of a constitutional monarchy or with meddling, democratically elected politicians.

The First World War should have been a chance for the Tsar of all the Russias to show the might of his empire. When war was announced, there were public demonstrations in favour of the tsar, proclaiming it would be a glorious triumph. The Russian army was the largest in the world and could rapidly bring 5 million soldiers into battle, at least theoretically. With such a mass of men, the Russian front should have swept forwards into Germany, but times had changed and sheer overwhelming manpower was no longer sufficient to guarantee victory.

At the outbreak of hostilities, the tsar was convinced to appoint his cousin, Grand Duke Nicholas Nikolaevich, as the commander-in-chief of the Russian forces. This seemed like a good idea at the time, as much of the day-to-day control of the war would remain with the generals anyway, and the grand duke had decades of military experience – though he had never actually been in a battle or commanded an army. In fact, when he received the orders to take command, Grand Duke Nicholas burst into tears and admitted he had no idea how to do the job he was being given.

The first months of the war saw several Russian armies almost completely wiped out due to strategic blunders. At the Battle of Tannenberg in 1914, swift movement by the Germans allowed them to halt and then destroy two Russian armies. Part of this success was due to the Russians not giving their orders over the radio in code, so the Germans simply had to tune into the right frequency to know where their enemy would be. In 1915, the Russians had to make a large retreat, abandoning territory, to prevent being encircled. Morale in the army was catastrophically low. Millions had already died, and those who were left to carry on the fight always struggled to have sufficient supplies delivered where they were needed. Something had to change.

It was at this point that the tsar made a fateful decision. He would himself become the commander-in-chief of his armed forces. With Tsar Nicholas II taking charge of his army he may have believed that his men would fight more bravely, since they were defending their divinely appointed ruler. He may also have felt that God almighty would not allow his anointed representative on Earth to suffer further defeats. In both calculations he was mistaken.

Tsar Nicholas moved out of Petrograd, as his capital and

seat of government had been renamed from St Petersburg to make it sound more Russian, to be closer to his troops. This was not strictly necessary, as the tsar never personally commanded any of his armies when he became the titular head of his forces. What his new position did, however, was tie each of the humiliating losses to the tsar himself. Every time land was given up to the enemy, it was the tsar who had to take responsibility. Every time a soldier saw a friend die bloodily in front of him, had to go days without bread, or found that he had no rounds for his gun, it was thanks to the ineptitude of the tsar. As millions of families were informed of yet another bereavement, they could point to the tsar as the man who had taken their sons from them.

The personal situation of the tsar did not increase his popularity among the populace. His wife, Tsarina Alexandra Feodorovna, was a German by birth, and many felt that she still harboured a secret fondness for her homeland and called for her to be deposed. With the tsar away from the capital, people thought that it was the tsarina who governed the empire in his name. Worse, the public believed she was under the malign influence of Rasputin, her own personal mystic. The tsarina's appointments of different ministers in rapid succession led to disorder in government and a perception that she was actively causing problems for the Russian command in the war.

RASPUTIN'S LEGENDARY DEMISE

Grigori Rasputin found favour at the Russian court because he claimed to have the ability to treat, through prayer, the haemophilia that threatened the life of Nicholas's only son, Alexei. Rasputin was eventually removed by an aristocratic plot that, it was claimed, saw the holy man poisoned, shot several times and thrown into the Neva River.

In 1917, the war became too much of a burden for Russia's creaking economy and government. The people were daily having to forgo food and other necessities of life to keep the armies at least partially supplied. Workers went on strike, and even the Duma, the usually docile parliament, called for the tsar to do something about these conditions. Nicholas responded by dissolving the Duma, and the Duma responded by forming a provisional government and insisting that the tsar abdicate. Nicholas duly signed his abdication, whereas his ancestors might have brought down bloody vengeance on them.

Tsar Nicholas II did not have long to enjoy his position as a former ruler of millions. In the communist revolutions that followed, the Romanov family became captives and were shuttled between various sites of imprisonment. On 17 July 1918, the story of Tsar Nicholas and his family ended in a barrage of gunfire in the basement of Ipatiev House, and their corpses were tossed in a mineshaft. The remains of most of the imperial family were only recovered in the 1990s.

SOVIET COLLECTIVIZATION KILLS MILLIONS

The Soviet communist government in Russia had come to power in the aftermath of the First World War with the promise of 'peace, land, bread'. The old regime of the tsars was one in which peasants were not much better off than the serfs who were tied to the fields they were forced to farm for wealthy owners, who often lived far away. The communists were implicitly promising that land would be redistributed more fairly and that there would be food and profit enough, for all.

The tumultuous birth of the Soviet Union came in the midst of a civil war between those who wanted change and forces seeking to restore the old order. To feed the workers and soldiers who kept the Soviet Union going, the government had been forced to requisition vast amounts of agricultural produce from farmers at a low price. This policy was ended once the civil war was won by the Soviets, but farmers did not get to enjoy their autonomy for long.

Joseph Stalin took over the reigns of government in 1924 and began a root-and-branch reorganization of the nation. The Soviet Union had inherited a ramshackle economy that was only barely industrialized. If the Soviet Union was to be able to compete with its more prosperous neighbours and potential enemies, then it would have to be brought into the modern age – whether its people agreed or not.

In 1928, Stalin unveiled his strategy for growth. The Five-Year Plan featured radical centralization of power over every aspect of the economy under the control of Soviet politicians. Energy production would be boosted, steel manufacturing would boom, and agriculture would be collectivized to produce bumper harvests. With these products, the Soviet Union could export goods to earn enough foreign currency to rebuild and modernize all aspects of the country. One Soviet book at this time told readers that the Soviet Union needed to earn gold to rapidly overtake capitalist countries and grow strong, so that it could free the workers of capitalist nations from their slavery to gold.

To feed the workers being dragooned into state service, in

1928 Stalin had to restart the seizure of grain from farmers. Naturally, the farmers resented this, and food production fell. Grain had to be imported into the Soviet Union from other nations, which drained the money reserves of the state. A furious Stalin blamed the shortfall on selfish farmers who were hoarding their harvests in a most uncommunist way. His wrath fell on the relatively prosperous farmers known as *kulaks,* who happened to own slightly more land than most. To stop the *kulaks* 'robbing' the state, a push was made to collectivize the farms of the Soviet Union.

By forcing farmers to pool their land into larger plots, it was hoped that they would become more efficient. The best farming practices could be employed to increase the yield of grain, which was vital to feeding the country and supplying foreign trade. The government could also make sure that the latest scientific and technological methods were being used, while state-owned modern equipment, such as tractors, could be moved between the collective farms. It would be a triumph of the proletariat coming together to work for the benefit of all. That, at least, was the theory.

It went wrong almost immediately. Farmers who had worked hard to improve their land and were getting the most produce were reluctant to share their bounty with others. No matter, those who refused to join were compelled by the threat of arrest or execution. Many farmers killed their livestock so that they could eat them rather than see them taken away – the numbers of all sorts of farm animals fell dramatically from 1929, when collectivization began. When the promised farm equipment failed to materialize, the farmers were still expected to grow as much as if it had been present.

The quotas of produce that the government expected were set very high to match the expectations that socialist policies in farming were bound to succeed. When these quotas were not met, Soviet authorities simply blamed the farmers for holding back supplies and confiscated as much as they could find, even if this did not leave enough for the farmers to eat. Soviet propaganda began to declare that the *kulaks* had to be destroyed by force, and posters showed fat farmers being beaten from the land.

Twenty-five thousand ideologically pristine industrial workers were selected to work on the farms and push up the harvests. Most had very little idea of how to farm and were not welcomed by the farmers, who saw them as agents of the government. Rumours flew among the farmers that the 'twenty-five thousanders' were there to spy on them and indoctrinate their children.

Ukraine was, and still is, the breadbasket of Europe, thanks to ideal conditions for growing grain. Opposition to the imposition of collectivization had been particularly strong there, and many Ukrainians wondered whether they might not be better off as a sovereign nation. In 1932, things came to a terrifying head during a period known as the *Holodomor* – a word meaning death by hunger.

LYSENKOISM VS DARWINISM

Science, when mixed with political doctrine, can produce terrible results. Trofim Lysenko was a pseudoscientist who rejected the capitalist notions of genetics. Using socialist theories, he believed he could breed hardier crops for the Soviet Union. Any scientist who disagreed with him was thought to be a traitor and risked death or imprisonment. When Lysenko's techniques failed to work, millions starved.

Famine reduced crop yields in 1932, and Stalin may have perceived this as a deliberate rebellion against his quotas. A decree known as 'Five stalks of grain' was promulgated, which declared that anyone, man, woman or child, who was found to have stolen any produce was an enemy of socialism and could be imprisoned or shot on sight. When this failed to increase the amount of food available, troops were sent to requisition any food that remained. This left farmers without food, so many of them turned to eating grass, acorns and pets. The misery spread. Cases of cannibalism were common.

The horror of the *Holodomor* cannot be overstated. Around 4 million people may have starved to death in the most horrible conditions. Today, it is regarded as a genocide committed against the people of Ukraine.

ALEXANDER FLEMING FAILS TO KEEP HIS SAMPLES CLEAN

The past was a terrifying place to live. Modern readers of old novels find it quaint that a chill could kill a heroine or that a person with tuberculosis might be sent away to the countryside to take the air. Before the invention of effective antibiotics, however, bacterial diseases were among the leading causes of mortality. A simple scratch could turn into a rotting sore that spread toxins around the body and put you in an early grave. A quick sexual dalliance could likewise be a death sentence if you contracted syphilis – which, before killing you, could cause your nose to rot away and destroy your mind.

Antibiotics thankfully changed all that, and today a handful of pills can cure many of the diseases that haunted our ancestors. In the early twentieth century, scientists had some success in synthesizing compounds that could treat some bacterial infections. But although Salvarsan, an arsenic compound introduced in 1910, was effective in treating syphilis, it had to be stored under nitrogen and had negative side effects.

The golden age of antibiotics truly began in 1928 with the discovery of the first naturally produced chemical able to kill bacteria: penicillin. Perhaps the most important discovery in the history of medicine, it was made through a mixture of accident and failure.

Alexander Fleming was a well-known bacteriologist, working at St Mary's Hospital in London, when he made his breakthrough. He had not been looking for an antibiotic by studying the bacterium *Staphylococcus aureus*. Fleming had simply prepared agar plates to grow his bacteria when an accident changed medicine forever.

In the common telling of the story, Fleming had left a window open while he worked, and a fungal spore from a study in a lab upstairs had floated in and landed on one of his plates. More likely, a spore came through an open door, as, despite working with some nasty bacteria, Fleming had a policy of always keeping his door open. Either way, Fleming put aside the plates of bacteria and went on holiday. When he returned, he was no doubt chagrined to find one of his bacterial plates studded with mouldy patches. In the normal course of events most scientists would have thrown the plate away and started again, but Fleming examined it and said, 'That's funny.'

Fleming had noticed that, while the rest of the plate was covered with bacterial colonies, there were clear areas around the fungus mould where no bacteria grew. It was as if something being produced by the fungus was killing the bacteria. Being a good scientist, he set about culturing the fungus, *Penicillium*, that had caused this remarkable effect, and repeated his experiment. Fleming was able to use extracts of the fungus, which he called 'mould juice', as an antibacterial. The active compound was named 'penicillin'.

The fact that there was now a way to treat everything from meningitis to diphtheria to gonorrhoea should have taken the world by storm; millions would be spared misery and death. Unfortunately, when Fleming announced his results and published them in a medical journal, hardly anyone took any notice. Some people have unkindly suggested that Fleming sat on his results and did nothing with them, but he did actually try to get people interested in what he had found.

However, there were difficulties in using penicillin as an antibiotic. It was an unstable molecule and difficult to isolate from the 'mould juice' that Fleming had been preparing. He was not a chemist, and had little experience in purifying organic compounds. Fleming had to move on to other work, but he sent out samples of his fungus to other labs, in case anyone wanted to follow it up.

With the Second World War raging, coming up with a drug that could treat bacterial illnesses became a priority. In 1939, Howard Florey, Ernst Chain, Edward Abraham, Norman Heatley and others conducted serious work in a lab in Oxford to turn a curiosity into a medicine. Their lab became a miniature factory for penicillin, with vast amounts of bacteria being tended by a group of six women who were dubbed 'the Penicillin Girls'. Within months, the team was able to show that mice that had been infected with bacteria survived when treated with penicillin, while those who were left untreated died. Soon, penicillin was being employed on the front lines and in hospitals around the world.

THE ANTIBIOTICS CAME FROM WHERE?!

The first patient to be treated with penicillin was a policeman called Albert Alexander, who in 1941 suffered a terrible infection of his face. For four days, he was injected with penicillin and seemed to improve, but then the researchers ran out of their drug. Despite managing to repurify some of the scarce compound from Alexander's urine to reinject it, Alexander died. Subsequent patients treated with improved supplies of penicillin were luckier and survived without having to have their toilets raided.

In 1945, Fleming, Florey and Chain were jointly awarded the Nobel Prize in physiology and medicine. There has been some controversy as to whether Fleming deserved his share, which came at the expense of other members of the Oxford team. After all, wasn't it a reward for the failure to keep a tidy and sterile lab? The greatest discoveries in science are often down to pure serendipity, though, and sometimes you just need to recognize a breakthrough when it happens, which Fleming had.

Medicine is a war between doctors and all the myriad ways in which our bodies can fail. We may be about to lose the battle against bacteria because of a failure to control the way antibiotics have been prescribed. Bacteria are not passive participants in this war and have evolved ways to survive antibiotics. The overuse and inappropriate application of antibiotics have enabled a range of infections to become increasingly resistant to them. Mass mortality from bacterial infection may not be a thing of the past after all.

Alexander Fleming himself foresaw the danger of antibiotic resistance. During his Nobel Prize lecture, he told the audience, 'The time may come when penicillin can be bought by anyone in the shops. Then there is the danger that the ignorant man may easily underdose himself and by exposing his microbes to non-lethal quantities of the drug make them resistant.'

CANE TOADS ARE UNLEASHED ON AUSTRALIA

· ·

In 2023, newspapers reported that a park ranger in Queensland, Australia, had stumbled on a monster creeping through the undergrowth. This may not have struck most readers as unusual, given Australia's reputation for being home to strange and dangerous animals, but the identity of the beast came as a bit of a shock. The park ranger captured what was found to be a record-breaking cane toad weighing 2.7 kg (nearly 6 lb), more than six times heavier than normal. Cane toads, not a native species, are one of the most destructive creatures ever to have reached Australia's shores.

The disastrous history of the cane toad, *Rhinella marina,* in Australia begins with a group of well-intentioned researchers who thought they had come up with an ingenious solution to beetle infestations that were damaging crops. Sugar cane was an economically important crop for Australian farmers, but the indigenous cane beetle did not respect farmers' fences. No sooner than the sugar cane was planted, cane beetles flew in and began to eat the leaves. Worse, they laid their eggs around the base of the plants, and their larvae burrowed down and ate the roots, killing the canes before they could produce their precious sugar.

The Australian authorities fought back against these pests in 1900 by sponsoring a series of Sugar Experiment Stations, where scientists could investigate methods of beetle-proofing the cane fields. Chemical warfare was the first attack tried against their beetle foes, but this proved ineffective, so the conflict was ratcheted up to include biological weaponry.

Towards the end of the nineteenth century, social, political and economic changes made the world feel significantly smaller. The finest minds set about improving the Earth by transplanting apparently advantageous species. Sometimes this was done to exploit a crop, as sugar cane was when it was introduced to Australia, but farmers often found that native species were able to destroy crops that had never evolved defences to their new neighbours, so sometimes a species was introduced to a new country to eradicate a pest species. This, it soon became apparent, could have unintended and terrible consequences.

In 1932, Arthur Bell attended a conference in Puerto

Rico, where he heard that the cane toad, native to Central America, was a voracious eater of insects and had been used to protect sugar cane fields. He captured some, brought them back to Australia, and set about breeding them. Eventually, thousands of cane toads were being held in special enclosures in Queensland, and, in 1935, two thousand four hundred were set free in the state.

This was a controversial move, as researchers had failed to ascertain whether the cane toads would actually eat cane beetles. Nor had they questioned how the introduced cane toads would interact with other native species. Voices raised against this hasty action included scientist Walter Froggatt, who wrote in 1936 that 'The great toad, immune from enemies, omnivorous in its habits, and breeding all the year round, may become as great a pest as the rabbit or cactus,' referring to two other damaging invasive species.

The release of cane toads was briefly banned, but the promise of an end to cane beetles proved too tempting, and soon more crates of toads were being dumped around the countryside. By 1950, as the effects of the toads' lifestyle were becoming better understood, this was widely acknowledged as a serious blunder.

Cane toads do eat cane beetles, but their diet is far wider than that, essentially including anything that can fit into their mouths, and the reptiles and amphibians that were already eating some of the cane beetles. Studies of sugar cane crop yields show that the introduction of the toads led to no significant increases. The burrowing larvae of the cane beetles were mostly ignored by the toads, who found there were far easier animals to prey upon. The cane toad population exploded in Australia, and today it is estimated to number around 200 million individuals.

THE GREAT, AND DISASTROUS, EMU WAR

In 1932, the Emu War began in Australia against the largest flightless bird on the continent. There were concerns that emus were destroying large numbers of crops, so an attempt was made to reduce their numbers. Major Gwynydd Purves Wynne-Aubrey Meredith set out with two machine guns to thin their numbers. It turned into a debacle, with hardly any emus killed and the military thoroughly embarrassed by the prowess of its avian enemy. The emus won this war.

The numbers of cane toads rose so dramatically because few native species could successfully consume them. The cane toad produces a toxin that coats its skin, so even handling the toads can cause a severe reaction, and any animal foolish enough to eat one is almost certain to sicken or die. The number of quolls, a type of carnivorous marsupial, plummets as soon as cane toads reach their territories, while other species find themselves competing with cane toads for prey. Wherever the cane toad inhabits sees a drop in biodiversity.

The government of Australia has attempted to fight back against the cane toad, but the advance of the toads is increasing. At present, the authorities are hoping for a ceasefire in the toad war, as they accept it is unlikely they can be fully eradicated. Methods are being trialled to protect populations of native species.

Japan Attacks Pearl Harbor and Causes a War it Cannot Win

· ·

On Sunday 7 December 1941, a date that will live in infamy, at a little before 8 a.m., waves of Japanese aircraft descended on the United States' Pearl Harbor naval base on Hawaii. Their aim was to cripple and destroy as much of the American Pacific Fleet as possible, so that the United States could not effectively strike back.

The road to the attack on Pearl Harbor had begun years

earlier, as the Japanese sought to create an empire in East Asia. Their bloody war against the Chinese saw them carve out large swathes of territory able to supply the labour and raw materials needed to feed their military machine. The Japanese still required huge amounts of imports to support their activities, however. The United States was officially neutral in this conflict, and Japan was one of the largest buyers of metals, oil and armaments.

The Roosevelt administration in Washington became concerned about the level of civilian casualties occurring in China and let it be known that selling aircraft and weapons to the Japanese would not be looked on favourably. These moralistic tones only got legal backing in 1940 when a new law was passed, which gave the president the right to control strategically important materials. The Second World War was presenting the very real risk of a complete takeover of both Europe and East Asia by militaristic regimes, so the United States had to prepare for a war.

When the Japanese invaded French Indochina to stop a flow of supplies to Chinese forces, the United States and United Kingdom responded with an embargo on all oil sales to Japan in 1941. A modern army, air force and navy run on oil, so if the supplies of oil ever ran out, the machines would grind to a halt. Japan drew up plans to invade the Dutch East Indies in order to seize their oil-producing capabilities. This was part of a wider planned invasion that would include an attack on the Philippines, which were under the protection of the United States. War seemed certain to follow if the Japanese made their move, and the American Pacific Fleet would be a major hazard to the overseas empire the Japanese were building. They believed their best hope was to remove the American Navy from the equation.

By November, a Japanese task force was sailing across the Pacific, which included carriers capable of launching hundreds of aircraft, and with them went submarines, battleships and destroyers. The Japanese government transmitted a declaration of war to the United States on the morning of 7 December, which was supposed to be delivered half an hour before the attack. The lengthy message, however, took too long to be decoded by workers at the Japanese embassy and was only handed over two hours after Pearl Harbor was targeted.

The first warnings of attack came when the USS Ward spotted an unidentified submarine approaching. Firing shells at it drove the submarine underwater, where it was destroyed with depth charges. Those onboard the USS Ward sent news of their actions to Pearl Harbor, but no one seems to have recognized that an attack was incoming. When a radar operator correctly interpreted a blip on his screen as launching aircraft he tried to inform his superiors, but was told they were away at breakfast. Being a Sunday morning, many were preparing for church services. At 7:51 a.m. the attack began.

Witnesses to the attack saw long lines of Japanese aircraft sweeping in low towards the ships moored in the harbour. Red flashes of tracer fire arched towards the incoming planes but could not hold back the assault, and the Japanese launched torpedo bombs, which holed the hulls of the battleships. Sailors caught by surprise by the sudden announcement of an attack found themselves rushing to their posts even as explosions tore through their vessels. Listing ships taking on water tilted sideways, leaving men scurrying desperately to reach the deck as water and oil pooled around them.

Once on deck, sailors could easily pick out the rising sun emblem of the Japanese Empire on aircraft strafing them at low altitude. One sailor remembered seeing a Japanese pilot giving him a mocking wave as he passed by. Bombs rained down on ships, submarine support buildings and planes. The oil spilled by the stricken ships caught fire, and soon it appeared that the entire harbour was aflame. Through the billowing smoke, the shrieks of dying comrades could be heard.

By the end of the attack, four American battleships had been sunk and four more heavily damaged, along with the loss of hundreds of aircraft caught on their landing strips.

Two thousand four hundred Americans lost their lives. The Japanese lost only twenty-nine aircraft. It must have seemed like a nearly complete victory for the Japanese Empire.

GERMAN DECLARATION

Germany and Japan had signed a treaty that specified that if either was attacked, then the other would come to their defence. Nothing in their alliance required them to join a war that the other had started. Germany did not have to declare war on the United States, but, four days after the attack on Pearl Harbor, Adolf Hitler announced, to the surprise of most of his military, that he was going to war with the United States. Historians have called this one of Hitler's biggest blunders, as America's power was soon turned on Germany.

The attack on Pearl Harbor was a failure, however. The Japanese assault had failed to target the infrastructure of the military base and the repair stations there, so Pearl Harbor was soon back in operation and able to work effectively for the duration of the war. By chance, the three aircraft carriers of the United States Pacific Fleet had been out of the harbour on sea manoeuvres at the time of the attack and so survived unscathed. The nature of naval warfare at this time was rapidly changing, and aircraft carriers would play a decisive role in the war to come. And it did come.

The United States had avoided becoming directly involved in the Second World War up to this point, but an attack on its fleet could not go unanswered. War was declared, and all of the might of the United States military and its vast economic resources were soon turned to defeating Japan. It would end in 1945 with two nuclear weapons destroying Hiroshima and Nagasaki, the unconditional surrender of Japan, and the dismantling of its empire.

Hitler's Wonder Weapons Waste Materials

The Second World War did not progress as Adolf Hitler had foreseen. Instead of his *Übermensch* warriors conquering the world, by 1942 they had become bogged down in Russia and had failed to knock Britain out of the war. The war had already been lost by the Axis powers – they just did not know it yet.

In Germany, increasing efforts were put into creating *Wunderwaffe*, 'wonder weapons', which would turn the tide of the war through Teutonic technological brilliance. Propaganda touted them as the silver bullets that would finally slay the Allied monster. Vast resources and expertise were invested into designing and building ships, tanks and missiles, all with incredible capabilities.

Some of the wonder weapons never got further than their initial designs. The Landkreuzer P. 1000 was a tank that, if built, would have weighed over a thousand tonnes. It was more like a battleship that moved on caterpillar tracks than a tank. Indeed, it would have been armed with guns only lightly modified from those used by the navy. Hitler became excited by the idea of this behemoth, despite the fact that it would have collapsed any bridge it tried to cross and would have been an obvious target for enemy aircraft. The project was cancelled before any of the tanks trundled, slowly, from the production line.

Other wonder weapons did see service, however. The Type XXIII submarine had an innovative design that allowed it to operate in coastal waters while remaining submerged at almost all times. After the war, many of its features would be adapted into more modern submarines, such as a fully welded single hull and large electric batteries. The problem with the wonder weapon programme was that when it finally led to usable products, they tended to come much too late to make any difference. The Type XXIII was only successfully used from 1944, and then in only small numbers.

The most famous wonder weapons were the *Vergeltungswaffen* – Vengeance Weapons. The V-1 was a flying bomb that consisted of a complex targeting system, a pulsejet engine that could push it to nearly 500 km (311 miles) per hour, and nearly a tonne of high explosives. They could be launched either from land or by plane. The whine of their engines became a familiar sound in the parts of England that were in range. Locals dubbed them Doodlebugs and soon learned that, so long as you could hear their engines, you were fine. It was once the engines cut out and the V-1 entered its death dive that you had to be afraid.

Terrifyingly, the V-1 could land almost anywhere, but while the mechanism for directing them was complicated, they could only be reliably targeted at an area with a diameter of 17 km (10.5 miles). Thousands of the V-1s fell on Britain, killing wherever they struck. Attacks by Allied aircraft on V-1 launch sites took valuable aircraft away from raids on more valuable Nazi sites. By some metrics, the V-1 programme, and its indiscriminate bombing of cities, was a success.

The V-2 rocket bomb, however, was a failure as far as the Nazi war aims were concerned. The V-2 was the first long-range guided ballistic missile and was a huge step forward in rocket design. While the V-1 could be intercepted by aircraft, the V-2 was blasted to supersonic speeds by its engine. You would only hear a V-2 after it had either passed overhead or reached its target. On impact, it detonated 900 kg (1,984 lbs) of explosives. The plans for the V-2 were perfected by 1943, and it was pushed into production.

By landing huge bombs in the heart of Paris and London, the V-2s were meant to destroy the morale of the Allied public and project a sense of the Nazis' futuristic power, but instead they were plagued by inaccuracy. They could explode harmlessly in fields, or drop on cinemas and kill hundreds. Despite the best efforts of Nazi ingenuity, most people living in the areas V-2s were striking simply carried on with their lives. It did not seem to matter much whether you were blasted to bits by a science-fiction weapon or a dumb bomb dropped by a plane.

Thanks to the use of double agents in Britain, the Allies were also able to direct some of the V-2s away from the capital. By telling the Nazis that their bombs were overshooting the city, the Germans were convinced to re-aim many of them to come down well before their intended target.

The true failure of the wonder weapons was their cost to the German economy. Simply designing the things took some of the brightest minds off work on German technological advances that might have been a real help to the war effort. Money and material that could have gone to the support of traditional warfare found itself squandered on projects that would never see the light of day, and have little effect even if they did.

The cost of building a single V-2 rocket was as much as that of a fighter aircraft, and was far more technically demanding. The rockets were powered by ethanol, which had to be distilled from potatoes, and with food in short supply in the final days of the war, this meant that essential sustenance was being fed into rockets rather than soldiers. Over a third of the alcohol in Germany was being drunk up by V-2s when it could have been used in other areas of industry.

THE BIGGEST GUN ON EARTH

The third vengeance weapon designed by the Germans was a battery of guns aimed permanently at London. Because of the required size, the guns had to be constructed in tunnels. The V-3 was built in the north of France and used multiple propellent stages to launch its shells. The V-3 was never fired, due to a raid by the RAF's 617 Squadron – better known as the Dambusters.

Perhaps the worst cost of developing the wonder weapons was the loss of life. While the V-2 rockets killed around nine thousand of their Allied targets, more than twelve thousand workers died during their construction, with many of the labourers tasked with building the rockets drawn from concentration camps.

When the war was ultimately won by the Allies, there was a curious race not to punish those who had designed the wonder weapons, but to hire them. Expert scientists from the Nazi regime were offered safe harbour in exchange for their expertise, an action known as Operation Paperclip in the United States. Wernher von Braun, head of the V-2 design team, went to the US, along with vast numbers of V-2 parts.

The V-2, when fired directly upwards, had been the first man-made object to be sent into space, and with the backing of the American government, von Braun built on his work to push for manned space flight. He was taken on by the newly formed NASA and led the development of the Saturn V rockets, which would be integral in carrying American astronauts to the moon. Despite his achievements, however, von Braun's presence in the US was controversial, given his Nazi past. One satirist mocked his passion for rockets in a cartoon that read, 'I aim at the stars, but sometimes I hit London.'

Sometimes a failure spawns a success. The V-2 was a disaster in terms of lives lost and cost to the Nazi regime.

Yet without the work of von Braun and scientists like him, it is unlikely that humanity would have entered the space age as soon as it did. Whether it was a price worth paying is a question we will continue to reckon with.

THOMAS MIDGLEY JR'S DISASTROUS GENIUS

. . . .

Every scientist hopes to leave behind a legacy of innovative discoveries that push forward human understanding and change the world. The spirit of Thomas Midgley Jr must have looked on with pride when a memoir of his life was published by the National Academy of Sciences in 1947, forever tying his name to four groundbreaking advances. His work on the vulcanization of rubber and extracting bromine from seawater strike us as impressive, but it is mainly for his two other discoveries that Midgley is best known today.

Thomas Midgley Jr enjoyed the fruits of his career while he was still alive. For his work in mechanical and chemical engineering, he had been feted by scientific societies and awarded numerous prestigious medals. Midgley first came to prominence when his interest turned to the problem of 'knocking' in motor engines during the First World War.

Knocking occurs when the fuel in an engine ignites at the wrong point in the piston stroke, and this causes a telltale knock or ping. As well as producing noise, the knocking reduces the effectiveness of the engine, and the increase in pressure at the wrong moment can actually cause the engine's destruction. It was a serious problem in an increasingly motorized world. A happy accident led to Midgley recognizing that a chemical additive to the fuel could reduce knocking. The question was, which one to use?

Midgley found many anti-knocking agents during his research. Tellurium turned out to have an unappealing smell, while compounds of antimony and arsenic were probably a little too toxic. The chemical he found to be most promising was tetraethyl lead. By adding just a little of this compound to gasoline, the phenomenon of knocking was finally removed as a danger to motors. Unfortunately, it turned out to be a real danger to humans.

Tetraethyl lead (TEL) was marketed as a miracle product. The dangers of working with lead compounds were already well known, but even the deaths of five workers in a factory making TEL did little to impede its popularity. The *New York Times* noted the controversy over TEL at the time, but in an editorial of 28 November 1924 concluded that the recent deaths were 'not a sufficient reason for abandoning the use of a substance by means of which a large economic gain could be effected

– that is, a considerable increase in the value of gasoline as a source of power.' The world seemed to agree that TEL was worth the risk, and the motor car took over the Earth.

It is impossible to say exactly how many millions of tonnes of lead were pumped into the atmosphere and environment by Midgley's creation of leaded fuel, nor can the effect on human health be fully known. By some estimates, perhaps 100 million deaths occurred prematurely due to increased levels of lead building up in human bodies. Millions may still be dying early each year, even though leaded fuels have mostly been phased out, due to residual lead in the environment.

Midgley was not content to rest on his laurels after his leaded fuel breakthrough. He knew that for refrigeration and air conditioning to become widely used, a new chemical refrigerant would need to be invented that did not carry the same risks of combustion as those used at the time. With little more than a pocket periodic table and a hunch, he concluded that any such compound would have to be built around fluorine, a ferociously reactive element. Midgley and his team soon created Freon, a form of chlorofluorocarbon. Chlorofluorocarbons would become known to generations as the dreaded CFC chemicals responsible for the destruction of the ozone layer.

CFCs are non-toxic when inhaled by mammals, so Midgley concluded that they were safe. The problem comes when they drift into the upper atmosphere, because CFCs catalyze a reaction that tears apart the ozone molecules that block many of the sun's harmful UV rays. Without the ozone layer, dangerous amounts of UV reach the Earth's surface and can cause skin cancers and cataracts. As an additional bonus, CFCs also contribute directly to global warming.

LEAD IN THE PIPES

Lead poisoning had been understood in the ancient world, with medical writers describing how those who worked with it suffered neurological symptoms. Yet lead pipes were used by the Romans to carry water. Some have blamed lead toxicity from the pipes for the fall of the Roman Empire, but research has debunked this. The Romans did, however, like to add lead acetate to wine as a sweetener.

Midgley cannot be solely blamed for the damage that his inventions did to the world. There were huge financial pressures for companies to use these products if they wished to stay in business. Businesses would also put pressure on legislators to stop the imposition of regulation, which might have phased out the use of lead in fuel and CFCs decades earlier than they did. Even when the role of others has been recognized, historians have still come to the conclusion that Thomas Midgley Jr is the single organism that has done most to harm the environment.

None of this was understood when Thomas Midgley died in 1944, so the inventor might have been content in his final moments. However, there was one last invention of Midgley's that had dire consequences for the man himself.

Midgley had been struck by polio in 1940, which left him without the use of his legs. Never one to despair, he turned his fruitful mind to creating a system of wires and pulleys attached to a harness that would allow him to get out of bed unaided. In 1944, Midgley was found dead from strangulation, after apparently becoming tangled in it.

STANISLAV PETROV FAILS TO FOLLOW PROTOCOL AND SAVES THE WORLD

Nuclear weapons are the most terrifying tools humanity has ever created, in a long history of discovering ever more sophisticated methods of slaughtering other humans. By harnessing the power of atomic fission, and later, fusion, atomic bombs are able to release enormous amounts of energy in an instant.

Their ferocity almost baffles the imagination. It is relatively easy to conjure up the damage that a single tonne of TNT would do if it detonated nearby, and that is catastrophic enough. The yield of nuclear weapons is measured in the kiloton range, equivalent to thousands of tonnes of TNT, or in the megaton range, equivalent to millions of tonnes of TNT. All of this explosive force is held in a bomb not much bigger than a fridge.

The first atomic weapons used in war were dropped by the United States on the Japanese cities of Hiroshima and Nagasaki, at the end of the Second World War. Accounts of the bomb dropping on Hiroshima revealed the dangers of nuclear warfare. Survivors saw a bright flash followed by a wave of pressure that knocked down houses, burying many people. This was followed by flames ignited by the intense heat of the blast. Witnesses saw the whole city erupting in flames and the destruction of 90 per cent of the buildings. Around eighty thousand people had been killed in an instant, sometimes leaving nothing more than an oily shadow behind as they vaporized. Soon the horrifying effects of radiation sickness developed on those exposed to the explosion, and all this was caused by what is now considered a relatively small atomic bomb of sixteen kilotons.

In the years following the end of the Second World War, a cold war developed between Western nations and the Soviet Union. An arms race was started between the blocs, which saw ever more atomic bombs being built and ever more powerful bombs being developed. By the late 1980s, there were more than sixty thousand nuclear weapons ready to be launched, most of them many times more powerful than the bombs dropped on Hiroshima and Nagasaki.

The governing philosophy of this build-up of atomic stockpiles was that having so many bombs would act as a deterrent to either side ever actually using them. Commonly known as Mutually Assured Destruction (MAD), the uneasy peace was maintained by fear that no one would survive if the nuclear powers attacked each other. There was no way to win a nuclear war. If even a single one-megaton bomb was detonated over the centre of London, New York, or Moscow, the entire city would be destroyed. At a distance of 30 km (19 miles) from the explosion, the flash of heat would burn flesh and ignite anything that could burn.

The world teetered on the edge of a nuclear holocaust for decades and several times came close to complete annihilation. If there was ever a nuclear attack, leaders would likely only have a few minutes to decide how to retaliate. Faulty detections of a launch nearly doomed humanity more than once. In 1960, the light of the moon tricked US radar stations into believing the USSR was attacking. Solar flares and even flocks of geese have also almost caused nuclear war, due to misidentification as incoming missiles. Yet, despite these near misses, nations remained on high alert, with missiles primed to fire. They had to be always ready to retaliate, as if they ever missed a real attack coming, they would not live long enough to regret it.

Soviet missile command was given the authority to launch its weapons on detection of an American strike because of the short amount of time that would have existed between seeing an attack coming and it landing. It was in the early hours of 26 September 1983 that a Russian satellite relayed its detection of a single American missile fired at Soviet territory. Stanislav Petrov was the man in charge that night of informing his superiors if there was any warning of an attack.

BROKEN ARROWS

The history of nuclear weapons is littered with close calls, where bombs were almost dropped due to faulty intelligence. Occasionally, nuclear weapons have been lost or been involved in accidents, in what the United States refers to as 'Broken Arrow' scenarios. When two US planes collided over Palomares in Spain in 1966, four bombs were dropped. Two of the weapons detonated the conventional explosives used to trigger the larger nuclear explosions when they struck the ground but failed to fully detonate.

Petrov found himself facing a computer screen and a blaring siren announcing that the Soviet Union was under attack. His orders were clear – he had to pass the message up the chain of command. No one would have questioned the need for the Soviets to launch their own weapons. Yet Petrov hesitated. He decided to ponder what the computer was telling him. Even as the system recorded four further launches, he considered what to do. Was it likely that if the United States decided to finally launch a nuclear war with the Soviets, they would send a handful of bombs when they had thousands at their disposal?

Instead of telling anyone that an attack was coming, Petrov telephoned his superiors and reported that there was a malfunction in the system. This may be the most consequential phone call in all of history, as it probably spared billions of lives. It was only twenty minutes later, when there were no reports of detonations, that Petrov could be sure that he had made the right decision.

Afterwards, it was confirmed that what the satellite had thought was the telltale flare of missile launches was in fact the glinting of sunlight off the tops of some clouds.

All of humanity must be thankful that Petrov failed to follow protocol. Almost any other officer on duty that night would have followed the set commands, which would have led inevitably to the complete destruction of the Western allies and the Soviet Union.

FAILURE IN COMMUNICATION
BRINGS DOWN THE BERLIN WALL

· ·

When Winston Churchill spoke of an Iron Curtain descending across Europe in the wake of the Second World War, he was speaking of an ideological divide between the Soviet and Western spheres of influence. As the Cold War deepened, the curtain hardened into a fixed barrier that severely restricted movement between the two worlds. Nowhere was this divide more concrete than in the city of Berlin.

After the defeat of Nazi Germany, different regions of the country were apportioned to each of the Allied nations. The Soviet Union was given the eastern part of Germany in which Berlin was situated, but instead of complete control of the city going to the Russians, Berlin was itself split up into Soviet, American, British and French sections.

In the 1950s, Joseph Stalin found the relatively free crossings between the east and west zones of Germany to be a security threat. He feared the entry of Western spies and saboteurs, as well as defections from the Soviets to the West. A heavily guarded border was erected that cut Germany in half. This left West Berlin, under Western control, as an outpost of capitalism within the Soviet Union. East Germans seeking to flee Soviet control could travel to West Berlin, and from there to West Germany. Millions took this path to freedom.

Tensions around the anomaly of Berlin continued until 1961, when Nikita Khrushchev ordered the closing of the border between East and West Berlin. On a day remembered as Barbed Wire Sunday, troops surrounded the 150 km (93 miles) around the western areas and began to build barricades. Roads were torn up to prevent the passage of vehicles. When it was realized what was happening, hundreds of thousands of Berliners turned out onto the streets to witness the events. A barrier was being made that would divide families on different sides of the border for decades.

A few East Berliners made audacious attempts to reach the West. Those who failed faced arrest at best, but could be killed by a hail of bullets at worst. People living in buildings that overlooked the border took the risk of jumping from their windows to try to land on the western side. Olga Segler was eighty years old when the barrier was constructed and found herself cut off from her daughter in West Berlin. With amazing bravery, she launched herself out of her window on Bernauer Straße to land in a net prepared to catch her, but instead of safety, she suffered a fatal injury. Several of her neighbours suffered the same fate after leaping towards freedom.

Over the following years, the barbed wire border was replaced by ever more secure barriers, including reinforced concrete, to prevent any breaches. To deter attempts to cross, the wall was alarmed, surrounded in places by ditches and well lit. From 1961 to 1989, thousands still tried to make their escapes west, but many found nothing more than an early death at the hands of guards who were rewarded for protecting the border with lethal force.

There are too many heart-rending tales that took place in the shadow of the Berlin Wall to chronicle, but one shows how desperate people were to cross to the West. In 1973, a pair of young parents decided to flee with their eighteen-month-old son, Holger. They concealed themselves in the back of a truck heading to West Berlin, but the truck was detained at the checkpoint for a long time. When Holger began to cry, his mother placed her hand over the child's mouth to quieten him. Unfortunately, Holger was suffering from an infection that left him unable to breathe through his nose. When the truck arrived in the west, the child's mother could do no more than hold out his lifeless body to rescuers.

By the end of the 1980s, the Soviet system of government was creaking and looking increasingly like it would fail. In November 1989, huge public demonstrations in East Berlin called for the resignation of the government and the liberalization of its policies. Perhaps a million people took to the streets. In an attempt to quell public discontent, it was decided that the method of obtaining a permit to cross into West Berlin would be made easier. On 9 November, a press conference was called, and Günter Schabowski made the announcement. Moments before he took to the stage, he was handed a note that was supposed to clarify the position of the East German authorities.

Schabowski was not fully aware of all the debate taking place at the highest levels of government about this policy and was unable to answer the questions posed by reporters. The plan had been for the policy to come into effect the following day, but when asked about when people could expect the change in travel permits to come into effect, Schabowski simply said that, as far as he knew, it was immediate. His failure to communicate the true intentions of the East German government to ease restrictions slowly rather than lift them entirely, gave demonstrators the encouragement they needed to march on the wall.

WALLPECKERS

In the aftermath of the Berlin Wall being opened, angry Berliners took their fury out on the structure that had for so long dominated their lives. They clambered onto the wall and used any tool they could find to begin tearing it to pieces. Their passionate smashing led to them being called *Mauerspechte* – wallpeckers.

Thousands of determined East Berliners crowded around the armed checkpoints that controlled passage across the wall and shouted to be allowed through. After all, Schabowski had said they were free to cross. The guards found themselves outnumbered and unable to reach superiors who could have given them direction, and no one wanted to fire into the crowd without authorization. The stand-off came to an end when one crossing commander opened the barriers. People streamed into West Berlin to see friends and relatives for the first time in years. The end of a dark phase of the Cold War came about because of confusion and misunderstandings.

AFTERWORD

No story is complete without a little sprinkling of failure. Every film must feature some setback to make the hero's eventual triumph all the more satisfying. If the failures in this book have depressed you, simply consider that the story is not over. For every failure that has been explored here, a million more could have taken its place. The history of humanity is the history of failure – and yet we are still here.

In some ways, failure is fundamental to life itself. Evolution only occurs because of accidental mutations that create diversity in a population, and what is a mutation except the failure of a cell to exactly copy its DNA? Without those fundamental failures, there would be no life more complex than single-celled organisms. Humans are a triumph of failure, and we are still here.

History should tell the whole story, but that is impossible.

One cannot include every fact of any narrative before it becomes bogged down in detail, yet even the smallest occurrence can transform everything that comes after it. By only focusing on successes and things that have turned out well, we produce a history that points towards our continual and inevitable perfection, but that is not the human story.

I hope this book makes you look at the failures in your own life a little more kindly. Nothing you do will probably ever earn you a place in the grand history of failure. And even if you mess up in a spectacular way, you can still try again. That's what humans have been doing for thousands of years – somehow, we are still muddling through.

ACKNOWLEDGEMENTS

Thank you first and foremost to my wonderful husband, Michael; you have stuck with me through all my failures and made me feel like a success. (He even forgives my failure to understand the difference between Girls Aloud and the Sugababes.) My family and friends have never failed to make me smile in the midst of a disaster, and they have supported me in too many ways to mention. Finally, I would like to thank everyone at Michael O'Mara Books for giving me the opportunity to write this book, especially Ross Hamilton and Louise Dixon for all their support and encouragement. Gabriella Nemeth has been an excellent editor and has rescued me from any number of blunders. Any failures that remain are a testament to my own fallibility.

SELECT BIBLIOGRAPHY

Reeves, Nicholas, *Akhenaten: Egypt's False Prophet* (Thames and Hudson Ltd, 2005)

Herodotus, trans. Aubrey De Selincourt, *The Histories* (Penguin Classics, 2003)

Stothard, Peter, *The Last Assassin* (Weidenfeld & Nicolson, 2020)

Murdoch, Adrian, *The Last Pagan* (Sutton Publishing Ltd, 2003)

Spencer, Charles, *The White Ship: Conquest, Anarchy and the Wrecking of Henry I's Dream* (William Collins, 2020)

Lomax, Derek W., *Reconquest of Spain* (Prentice Hall Press, 1978)

Cook, Noble D., *Born to Die: Disease and New World Conquest, 1492–1650* (Cambridge University Press, 1998)

Hutchinson, Robert, *The Spanish Armada* (Weidenfeld & Nicolson, 2014)

Schama, Simon, *Citizens: A Chronicle of the French Revolution* (Penguin, 2004)

McMeekin, Sean, *The Russian Revolution: A New History* (Profile Books, 2018)

Brown, Kevin, *Penicillin Man: Alexander Fleming and the Antibiotic Revolution* (The History Press, 2005)

Nelson, Craig, *Pearl Harbor: From Infamy to Greatness* (Weidenfeld & Nicolson, 2018)

INDEX